HEADHUNTING

HEADHUNTING

A GUIDE TO EXECUTIVE SEARCH IN ASIA

Dr Stephanie Jones

World Executive's Digest

THE MAGAZINE FOR
MANAGEMENT
EXCELLENCE

Prentice Hall

First published 1995 by
Prentice Hall
Simon & Schuster (Asia) Pte Ltd
317 Alexandra Road
#04-01 IKEA Building
Singapore 159965

 Published by Simon & Schuster (Asia) Pte Ltd
A division of Simon & Schuster International Group

Cover photograph by Richard Wahlstrom and The Image Bank

Printed in Singapore

2   3   4   5   99   98   97   96

ISBN 0-13-183385-5

Prentice Hall International (UK) Limited, *London*
Prentice Hall of Australia Pty. Limited, *Sydney*
Prentice Hall Canada, Inc., *Toronto*
Prentice Hall Hispanoamericana, S.A., *Mexico*
Prentice Hall of India Private Limited, *New Delhi*
Prentice Hall of Japan, Inc., *Tokyo*
Editora Prentice Hall do Brasil, Ltda., *Rio de Janeiro*
Prentice Hall, Inc., *Upper Saddle River, New Jersey*

CONTENTS

Foreword by John C. C. Chan, Managing Director, Kowloon Motor Bus vii

Foreword by the Editor-in-chief of *World Executive's Digest*   ix

PART ONE   INTRODUCTION

Chapter 1   Introduction   3
Chapter 2   Introduction to Executive Search   11
Chapter 3   The Economics of Search   20

PART TWO   EXECUTIVE SEARCH IN ASIA, MARKET BY MARKET

Chapter 4   Hong Kong – Home of International
                  Executive Search in Asia   29
Chapter 5   China – The Greatest Recruitment
                  Challenge in Asia   58
Chapter 6   Taiwan – More Mobility, Especially with
                  the China Connection   69
Chapter 7   Singapore – Still a Land of Opportunity   78
Chapter 8   Malaysia – Relaxation of Work
                  Permit Restrictions   86
Chapter 9   Thailand – Only Thais Need Apply   95
Chapter 10   Philippines – Go Overseas to
                  Seek Your Fortune   105
Chapter 11   Indonesia – Opening up to
                  Foreign Investment   115

PART THREE THE EXECUTIVE SEARCH PROCESS

Chapter 12	Examining the Search Process	129
Chapter 13	An Executive Search Case Study	151

PART FOUR CAREERS AND EXECUTIVE SEARCH

Chapter 14	Hints on How to Get Headhunted	171
Chapter 15	Career Moves through Headhunting	180
Chapter 16	Becoming an Executive Search Consultant	186
Appendix	Careers in Asia	190
Glossary		202
Index		208

FOREWORD

by John C. C. Chan, Managing Director, Kowloon Motor Bus, Hong Kong

Headhunting is relatively new in Asia, but it is now a significant part of corporate life here, and Hong Kong is, I believe, the place where executive search in Asia is most well-developed and advanced, and has the greatest market penetration.

Yet many people who come into contact with headhunters – both those being headhunted and those using headhunters – are fairly unclear about what headhunters actually do. For example, some still believe that executive search firms will find you a job, when actually they do not work on behalf of individuals, but only work as instructed by corporate clients.

Dr Jones' book is therefore timely and appropriate, with fascinating details and useful explanations. Even for those like myself, who have both been headhunted and use headhunters, this book contains a lot to be learnt about making the most of this potentially important connection. Everyone needs advisors in planning their careers and in running their businesses. Headhunters can play a significant role in both.

I have been headhunted several times during my career, first in the Hong Kong Government and later in the corporate sector. Now I frequently find myself on the other side of the fence – as a client of search firms. As a steward of the Royal Hong Kong Jockey Club, a council member of the University of Hong Kong, and on the council of the Hong Kong Stock Exchange, I am frequently involved in high-level search assignments.

So I see the value of search firms in both being headhunted and in doing headhunting. In the case of the former, I see headhunters as playing a part in maintaining the confidentiality of your job move, and of giving you unique insights into the company you're considering joining. They can also help avoid embarrassment by conducting salary negotiations on your behalf. In using a search firm to recruit a top manager, you can cast the net wide, especially in international recruiting. Through the search firm, you can obtain detailed information on each candidate before you meet him or her. Using a search firm takes some personal scruples out of the appointment process – they make the whole business of hiring more objective and professional.

It seems to me that most of the movements of top people in Hong Kong nowadays are the result of headhunting activity. These sort of people are too busy to read job ads. I never do. They will consider new opportunities only if personally approached. And search activity in Hong Kong is escalating with the run-up to 1997. There's an increasing focus on top-notch people of Chinese race (or people of any race who speak Chinese, and understand China), and there is only a small pool of these people. Meanwhile, demand is rising steadily, as few now doubt that this is the Asia Pacific decade. With this scenario as a backdrop, headhunters will continue to flourish, and companies and individuals can reap the benefits.

For running a major Asian business like Kowloon Motor Bus (founded in 1933, with 11,500 employees and a turnover of HK$3 billion), people are our principal asset. This sounds clichéd, but it's true. Our senior managers literally keep the company on the road. Finding them, hiring them and keeping them occupies a lot of the attention of myself and my top management team, and this also goes for the other companies and organisations with which I am associated. Especially at the most senior level, headhunters make our life easier and have enabled us to attract people of a calibre we couldn't necessarily identify on our own.

I recommend Dr Jones' book most warmly to senior executives in Asia and all those doing business in Asia who are building up their senior management teams across the region – and all those on the move!

John C. C. Chan, CBE, LVO, JP
Managing Director
Kowloon Motor Bus

FOREWORD

by the Editor-in-Chief of *World Executive's Digest*

World Executive's Digest readers are known for having important management responsibilities and being significant decision makers in their companies. And as we have seen time and again in the pages of our magazine, one of the greatest issues facing Asia's managers today is identifying and attracting the very best fellow managers.

At the same time, *World Executive's Digest* readers are clearly upwardly-mobile, and never miss an opportunity when it comes to building on career opportunities. So we felt that our new series, launched in January 1993, was particularly appropriate. *The WED Guide to Executive Search in Asia,* on which this book is based, is the first of its kind, when executive search is gaining maturity and a greater presence in the region.

Before joining us, our Academic Editor and Hong Kong Bureau Chief, Dr Stephanie Jones, wrote *The Headhunting Business* (about executive search in the United Kingdom), her all-time bestseller. She is clearly one of the most appropriate people to write this series for us.

We are delighted that Simon & Schuster have published our series in book form. Dr Jones has incorporated a good deal of new material into the book, so we urge *WED* readers to buy it, even if they have faithfully kept all their back issues!

Executive search is a fascinating world which feeds on fast-moving information and keeping ahead of the game. The headhunters, working with many of Asia's most important companies – both local and multinational – know details of corporate strategies before anyone else does.

If a company is moving into China, for example, it must have the experts in place before it can make a move. In another example, if a company is diversifying into a new product area, then the first task is to go out and hire a product-development director. If one company wants to take over another, often it will hire key managers to run the new company – even before they've bought the first share.

Companies can love executive search firms and hate them too. They can find you the man – or woman – to lead your company from disaster to recovery, but they can also tempt away your best staff if you can't keep them. Some companies keep search firms on retainer in an attempt to make sure that their key people are off-limits.

Search is now here to stay, and whether you want to hire headhunters yourself for your senior recruitment needs, get headhunted or join their ranks, you need to know who they are and what they do. This book will let you into their secret world! I do hope you enjoy it and find it a positive help in your career.

Jet Magsaysay
Editor-in-Chief
World Executive's Digest

PART ONE

INTRODUCTION

CHAPTER 1

INTRODUCTION

Over the last decade, executive search has played an increasingly prominent role in the appointment of executives into key management positions across Asia. Representatives of large international search firms first came to Asia following their clients, mostly fast-growing American and European multinationals. Since then, two important developments have taken place: these firms have built up significant domestic client-bases, including Singaporean, Hong Kong Chinese, Malaysian and other local Asian companies using search for the first time; and they have new competitors in the form of recently emerged indigenous search firms. In this book, we concentrate mainly on the major international firms, although we do refer to smaller firms and independents in our market studies.

Executive search, or 'headhunting' as it is more informally known, is now a complex and highly sophisticated business. In the United States and in much of Europe, over 75 per cent of all senior executive placements are the result of executive search activity. There are still cultural barriers preventing such a widespread usage of search in Asia at the moment, but it is probably just a question of time before the practice becomes more generally accepted.

EXECUTIVE SEARCH FIRMS

In this book, we present market reports of search activity with critical reviews of international and local search firms operating in the region. The firms included here have many of these features in common:

* All these firms operate on behalf of companies seeking senior personnel ONLY. They are hired by organisations looking for help in identifying and attracting key personnel, and NEVER accept payments from people looking for a job. They are interested in individuals who are active on the job market only in so far that they may become candidates for present or future headhunting assignments.

* Most of these firms operate on a retainer basis only; generally, they are paid a significant proportion of their fees on agreement of the headhunting assignment, and receive further payments as the search progresses, but these are NOT, in most cases, contingent on the placement of a candidate in the job. In the United States and elsewhere, headhunting firms are divided between 'retainer' and 'contingency'; this is an important distinction for the user of search and for job seekers.

* Most of these firms have a significant presence in the Asian market, operating from at least two centres in the region. These centres are used as a base to cover other countries, where offices may be established when demand is sufficient.

* Many of these firms are members of large international search firms, with the capability to search for candidates across the United States, Europe and other regions, including Australasia.

In some of our market reports, especially where executive search is comparatively undeveloped, we also look at selection activity, that is, the use of classified advertising to attract candidates who are then interviewed and shortlisted and then presented to the client. But most of the above points still apply: we look at firms working on behalf of clients, on retainer, with a presence in more than one centre. Many of these are international accounting or management consulting firms.

WHERE ARE THE SEARCH FIRMS IN ASIA?

In Asia (in this book we are excluding Japan and Australia), international search firms initially established bases in Hong Kong, spreading out from there according to client demand. The most popular base for a second Asian office has been Singapore, followed by Bangkok; China is looking promising for the future. As yet, no major international search firm except Korn/Ferry and Boyden operate in Thailand, and none of these firms have yet entered the Philippines, although some have affiliations. Kuala Lumpur and Jakarta are now being targeted as important centres for possible future search activity.

The most attractive locations for executive search are seen as those with a growing presence of major multinationals, a high level of demand for executives, and high salary levels. Hong Kong has been especially successful, not just because of the existence of many large international companies, but because there is a tradition of career mobility among both the expatriate community and the local Chinese population. It has been relatively easy to establish an acceptability of headhunting within Chinese executive circles in Hong Kong (especially among the growing number of Chinese executives educated in the United States), but this is less the case in Japan, where executive search operates in total contravention to accepted practices of 'lifetime employment' and considerable adhesion to the concept of company loyalty.

Search consultants are now being employed by several family-owned companies in Asia, especially when they feel a need for professional executive talent to operate on their behalf internationally. But this is a big step for them to take. To do their job properly, search consultants need insights into their client company in order to 'sell' the opportunity and represent their needs, and not all Asian companies are used to divulging corporate confidences to external consultants. Yet there are signs that this is changing, with Hong Kong-based Chinese companies taking a lead here.

WHY SHOULD YOU KNOW ABOUT SEARCH?

The fact that search is gaining a more widespread presence in Asia, both in terms of the number of companies using search firms and in terms of the countries into which search firms are penetrating, means that all fast-track executives looking for enhanced career opportunities should know the names of the major firms operating in their region and, more significantly, should know the names of the key consultants working within them. Preferably, they should make themselves known to them personally.

They should also know the difference between retainer and contingency search firms, and how to make the distinction between executive search (using research to identify candidates and then making approaches to them) and executive selection (using advertising to attract candidates and then sifting the responses).

Knowing about search firms can be valuable to executives for four reasons, which we will discuss in more detail later. First, search firms can be hired by the executive's company to track down and attract a senior manager to help the company to implement a major new policy, or to fill a vacancy left by a departure or retirement. Second, executives can use search for networking and to make themselves available for new career opportunities. Third, by acting as 'sources' to executive search consultants and referring names, executives can recommend others whom they think are outstanding in their field, and they can gain a reputation for knowledge and judgement. Finally, executives may also be interested in becoming headhunters themselves at some stage in their careers.

HOW EXECUTIVE SEARCH WORKS

Basically, the client approaches the search firm with a more or less specific need. The client may have used the firm before, have heard about it, or may have staged a competitive pitch between rival firms for the assignment. The client and the consultant(s) who will work on the search agree on the nature of the job, and the places where candidates may come from, both in terms of other companies, industries and/or geographical locations. There will be some discussion of the salary and bonus requirements. They will agree on the firm's fee, based either on one-third of the successful candidate's first-year remuneration and bonus, or a flat fee based on the expected time the search will take and the difficulty of the assignment. The dates when the fee installments are to be paid will also be agreed. Although many firms in Asia act on a contingency basis, with most of the fee coming only after the placement of the successful candidate, this book concentrates on retainer-based search.

The search consultant – with help from their firm's research department, and through 'sourcing' – will identify a 'long list' of candidates, to be reduced down to a 'short list', and will present the most suitable candidates to the client, having interviewed them and prepared reports on them and the market as a whole. The client meets the shortlisted candidates and decides. It may be that the search consultant must return to the long list, or start a new search in a different area. Retainer search firms commit themselves to the successful outcome of the search. If the candidate who has been placed leaves or is dismissed within six months, a search will start for the successor without a further fee.

Ultimately, the successful candidate is appointed, with the consultant helping in the salary and bonus negotiations, and other terms and conditions. Normally the consultants will also monitor the success of the placement, keeping in touch with both the client and candidate for the next few months.

Being a Search Firm's Client

As a client of a search firm, you must know the right questions to ask, and to be convinced of the reliability, integrity and reputation of that firm in the market. You should have a clear idea of the sort of person you want, but also be prepared to listen to their comments and suggestions. You must constantly be aware of their progress during the search process, and make yourself available to meet them and meet the candidates in due course. You must feel content that the firm you have chosen – and the consultant(s) working for you – fully represents your interests and can act as your ambassador outside the company. You must be able to trust their judgement and knowledge in putting forward ideal candidates, but not allow yourself to be influenced too closely by whom they suggest. You should ask to see background research and to know more about the total population of people approached on the search. You should feel satisfied that the market has been thoroughly explored and that the search consultant has done everything possible to secure the best outcome.

Being the Search Firm's Candidate

As a candidate, you should know how to respond when you receive that telephone call: ask to speak to the search consultant later, at home, when you won't be disturbed by colleagues, and meanwhile you should check that they are a reputable firm used to dealing with top clients, handling the sort of opportunities in which you might be interested.

If you are looking to move to another company, you should keep your CV or résumé up to date, and make sure that the most appropriate search firms have a copy on file. Try to meet them if you can, either by approaching them cold or, preferably, by gaining an introduction through a mutual friend or associate. In discussing your career and future plans, be as candid as possible and, during an assignment, put your cards on the table. Never pretend to be interested when you are not. Search consultants and their clients don't like surprises, and one of the greatest difficulties impeding successful searches is the tendency for a number of candidates to change their minds about moving and stay with their old job, especially when offered financial inducements to stay.

Being the Search Firm's Source

Some people think that every time a search consultant calls, they're being offered a job. This is rarely the case. Certainly, there will be other candidates involved, and in many cases the consultant will be asking for your advice only. You are being 'sourced', or asked to suggest names. It is a good idea to make yourself useful to him or her in this respect, because then you will almost certainly be regarded in a favourable light for opportunities more suitable to you, and this will help you to gain a reputation for knowledge and judgement in your field. Word will rapidly spread around the grapevine that you suggested the person who was placed in a key job, for example, and this will do no harm to your personal reputation for influence and expert insight. No search consultant should ask you to recommend an existing colleague, because you would not be expected to be so disloyal to your company, but instead you may be asked about people you worked with in a different company, or in a trade association. You may also find yourself being sourced whilst search consultants carry out reference checking on their most likely candidates.

Becoming a Search Consultant Yourself

At the end of this book, as you read about the different search firms and how they are operating across Asia, you may feel that you might enjoy being in this business yourself, especially if you have met a number of search consultants whilst looking to change jobs, or if you were placed by a search firm. A number of search consultants have previously worked in personnel and human resource-related jobs. Ideally, they should have had substantial management experience to be able to relate to the sort of people their clients hope to attract. It is also possible to enter the search world after management experience and then return to the outside world when an ideal opportunity arises. Search gives an insight into a variety of different career opportunities. A career in executive search certainly has a lot of variety and autonomy and a degree of satisfaction, although few consultants publicly announce that they were responsible for a particular placement.

Consultants must be highly discreet and able to deal with confidential information; they must be persuasive, determined and able to keep an assignment going, even in the midst of problems. The most successful are well qualified academically (MBAs are popular) and have held important management positions, usually in different companies, and often in different countries.

HOW THE SEARCH FIRMS AND MARKETS WILL BE ANALYSED, AND WHY

In this book, we will be looking at search in Asia in two aspects: firms and markets.

Firms

We shall be examining four of the major international wholly owned search firms based in Hong Kong and operating around the region. We shall be covering these points:

* When each firm was founded in Asia, the number and location of offices

* The numbers of consultants

* The sectors of industry in which the firm specialises, and the management positions they most frequently fill

* The average salary per assignment over last year

* The number of assignments the firm carries out per year

* The backgrounds of the individual consultants, and how knowledgeable they are about certain industries, and their ability to relate to senior executives

* The industry sectors and positions currently in most demand

* The changes in supply and demand over recent months or years

* Their advice to aspiring executives wanting to be headhunted

* The proportion of different nationalities among candidates

* The proportion of women among placements

* The extent to which they work with expatriate clients/candidates or locals

* The amount of work they do in other locations across Asia, in terms of carrying out assignments for local companies, and in using other countries as a source of candidates

❋   How important they judge academic qualifications to be and why they feel they are particularly special, compared with their competitors

We will also be talking to clients of these firms, and executives they approach as candidates and sources. How do the different firms compare? Although they are in the same business, all users and candidates comment on the different styles and approaches of the different firms.

Markets

We shall be examining the executive search markets around the region, covering the following points, with some variation according to the special circumstances of some markets:

❋   How widespread the use of search is in each market

❋   The names of the principal search firms operating in the market

❋   The sectors of industry and functional positions in most demand

❋   The average salary per search assignment

❋   Advice to executives looking for career opportunities in this market

❋   The experience and qualifications of candidates here

❋   The client-base of search firms – expatriate or local

❋   The proportion of women among placements

❋   Other countries as a source of candidates

❋   Competitive differentiators between firms

❋   Client comments

❋   The nature of selection activity here

Our aim will be to provide enough information for you to be able to compare firms critically, and to know how to relate to them and work with them, as a client, a candidate, a source or as a potential search consultant yourself; and to understand the differences between different Asian countries and cities as recruitment markets, and the firms operating in them, both in executive search and selection.

CHAPTER 2

INTRODUCTION TO EXECUTIVE SEARCH

What is executive search? To what extent is it taking off in Asia, and what are the problems? What roles do search firms play? Why and how do companies use search to recruit managers?

Executive search can be a very effective, professional, objective and discreet way of hiring senior managers in key positions; but it is expensive, for high-level personnel only, and employers using this option must be very careful to hire only a reputable search firm. Search is well established in the United States and Europe, where many of the less reputable operators have now been weeded out, especially during the hiring recession of the last few years. In Asia, search is still relatively new, is confined to the largest and most mature business centres, and has attracted scores of possibly dubious operators who nevertheless insist on calling themselves executive search consultants. Using search effectively requires knowledge of the way that search firms should operate, and of the particular firms which have established a track record in Asia.

Researching the use of executive search is very difficult. The search firms will not reveal to outsiders who their clients are, and companies questioned about their search usage tend to give few details. However, it is possible to ascertain the popularity of search as an option for recruiting managers by looking at the levels of activity of search firms. How busy are they? Are they gaining more and more clients? Are they doing more and more work for their clients? We can also look at the advantages and disadvantages of using this approach to solve the problem of the shortage of managers.

We will see in the market reports in Part Two that search is becoming well established in Asia, particularly in Hong Kong, but this level of search activity is not uniform across the region, nor is it as sophisticated and understood.

Using executive search to import managers across borders in Asia can often be difficult. An international search firm, with branches across Asia, quotes the example of the search consultant who was stopped at the Customs in Taipei and asked "Who were you seeing? Why?", as the Taiwanese authorities were becoming concerned that search was being used to approach people in government agencies to attract them to private sector positions. This kind of activity can rebound on the company giving out the search assignment, who can have their work permit taken away. For example, sanctions were brought against a major US bank talking to a banker in the government reserves department in Taipei.

So international search firms are not necessarily opening branches all across Asia. Instead they tend to make short visits and/or ask candidates to come to them in Hong Kong or in Singapore, from Taiwan, Indonesia and the Philippines, rather than setting up a base there themselves. Thailand and Malaysia are, to a certain extent, exceptions, as the business communities there are becoming more diverse in terms of attracting multinationals, and salaries there have now reached such levels that it can pay to have an office there.

USE OF SEARCH IN CERTAIN SPECIFIC AREAS

A typical executive search consultant in Singapore reveals that in his experience, search is most used in certain functional areas, "such as (in financial services) for private bankers, foreign exchange traders, corporate financiers and (in financial services and other sectors) human resources professionals in a regional context, and financial controllers, and executives in tax planning, treasury, information technology, marketing and pharmaceuticals." The functional positions and business areas which dominate the activity of most search firms often indicate those in greatest demand and shortest supply. We look at these in each of our market reports. Also, the use of search can indicate shifts in national economies. According to this headhunter,

> the use of executive search for regional jobs out of Singapore, which is now becoming increasingly important as a regional centre thanks to government encouragement, the high costs of locating in Tokyo, and uncertainty over the future of Hong Kong. Regional jobs in most demand include human resources directors, finance directors, and marketing directors.

THE ROLES OF THE SEARCH FIRM

Search Firms as Repositories of Available Managers

Many search firms around the region receive thirty to forty unsolicited CVs/résumés ('write-ins') a day in each office, and 10 per cent get onto shortlists, compared with only 1 per cent or 2 per cent in the United States and Europe. In Asia, it is well worth executives' time in networking through executive search in this way. These executives who know how to network through search send their résumés in to more than one firm to widen their options. They also know which firms and which consultants are most interested in their areas of specialism.

Search Firms as Sources of Information about the Job Market

Many search consultants talk of expatriate packages disappearing. On average only about 12 per cent of candidates are expatriates. But there are still important reasons for hiring them, such as the fact that in many Asian cities, Europeans or Americans are seen as neutral and useful for such roles as Human Resources director, for example. Many headhunters also find that women executives are increasingly making the grade, and they are seen as especially popular for positions in finance, banking and IT. In the region as a whole, nearly 50 per cent of all executives in Human Resources (HR) are women, and this is especially true for Singapore and Hong Kong. Overall, up to 30 per cent of candidates in Singapore are female, according to one prominent firm there. The hiring of women can help solve the problem of the shortage of managers, and search is one way of targetting them. In a very tight job market, search consultants can provide invaluable advice on the levels of salaries necessary to attract key people, and the likelihood of being able to fill positions swiftly or satisfactorily.

HOW TO RANK SEARCH FIRMS TO HELP IN CHOOSING BETWEEN THEM

This can be done by revenues, on the grounds that firms doing well must be effective, but in Asia revenue figures can be misleading. If a firm is operating on behalf of a multinational client (as they are in most cases), they can be paid offshore to be more tax efficient, and not reveal these revenues.

Ranking can also be carried out by reputation, by asking other users about satisfactory service from search firms, especially in the context of how long placements stay in their jobs, and how often the firm has to repeat a search to find a candidate who will 'stick'. Users of search should also look at independent operators as well as the large, international firms (especially those consultants who were once with large, international firms and have now left to start up on their own).

Warnings for Users of Search

Users of search should also be careful of the use of the word 'search', as this is often applied to any form of advertising of job vacancies. Some agencies, calling themselves 'executive search firms', simply offer résumés to employers on a contingency basis. There is no regulation of the search market in Asia, and users and prospective candidates should check bonafides, and executives should be warned against talking too readily to consultants and recruiters they don't know. Above all, when they are approached any potential candidate must make sure that the search firm has a retained assignment, and is not trying to fill a known need speculatively.

Users should also check the level of the appointment with those typically handled by the search firm, to make sure they are matching the level of the firm with the level of the post to be filled (some search firms have selection/advertising sections which can handle lower-level assignments more effectively).

THE INPUT OF HEADHUNTERS TO A COMPANY

Why use headhunters? The reasons for using some form of external assistance in recruiting key people are often quite clear: the confidentiality, the know-how and the experience are all obvious factors; why bring in a headhunter rather than use an advertising consultant is sometimes more difficult to explain. Often a headhunter will advise the client to advertise if in his or her judgement it is the most appropriate way of identifying and recruiting suitable people. The last thing an executive search consultant wants to do is to take on an assignment which is not achievable and which he or she cannot complete. No one is going to be happy with that situation. The job has to be at a level senior enough and the number of people who could do the job restricted enough to enable the job to be open to search. If there are potentially 5,000–10,000 people who can do the job, then it is almost certainly more appropriate to advertise, perhaps anonymously.

However, when the market is clearly defined and there is a limit to the number of people who could do the job, then talking to a headhunter may well be the best first step, once internal candidates have been considered. Executive search is one of those products which has a large degree of elasticity. That is, the person who is selling the product and service can persuade potential clients to buy the service, and it is only really limited by the quality of people selling the service.

A good headhunter should have significant awareness of how other companies have solved each recruitment problem, and knowledge about the market-place in which to look for an individual. Often, if they have a disposition to broader problem solving, the search consultant can provide his/her view on several issues:

* The potential organisational structure

* How the individual would fit in

* The likely scope of his or her responsibilities

* If the tasks he or she will be set are manageable

* If candidates can be found in the market who meet this particular specification

* Whether the search can be a local search or needs to be regional or international

* Whether any of the top candidates can be attracted for the remuneration offered, or whether or not the remuneration of the senior team needs reviewing

❋　If the nationality of the candidate is important

❋　What happened to the last job holder in this case, if he or she moved onto a bigger job after some success, or was fired

The headhunter may well feel that there is a need to bring a more general consulting focus to bear in order to solve the organisational issues before an executive search is undertaken. Sometimes the consultant feels that there is so much ambiguity regarding the appointment that it is unlikely to be successful as presently structured. There may well be differences of view among board members on the matter of the type of person required and the future role. A good executive search consultant can help resolve those issues, often working with and alongside the chairman and managing director (MD). Sometimes the headhunter receives a fee for that advice without even undertaking an executive search. Some companies simply use search consultants to give an opinion on the quality and standing of their executive group.

In Asia, especially in the more mature search markets such as Hong Kong and Singapore, there is evidence of a wider use of search firms beyond simple recruitment assignments.

EXECUTIVE SEARCH AND CHANGING ORGANISATIONAL STRUCTURES

In the 1990s, the internal departments and head office staff of many organisations – especially multinationals – are a lot smaller than they were in the 1970s and 1980s. In fact, many organisations have reduced this and other functions to such an extent that they use consultants for a wide variety of activities whether it be for strategic advice, for marketing, production, organisation development, training or indeed executive search.

If there is a relationship with existing search firms, the client may well use such a known firm when making further appointments. If there are doubts about the search firm's ability to work at a senior level, say to find a chief executive, the client may well invite two or three firms in to pitch competitively and see who has the best overall track record and appears most attractive and experienced to the board.

Search at Different Levels

Companies using search are becoming aware of the relevance of search in different levels within an organisation and, if they have a smaller headhunting firm working at one level in the organisation, they may well not use that firm when a very senior appointment arises. This is why, in a large number of instances, the major, large executive searches go to the top firms rather than those that are smaller. It is one thing to trust a middle management appointment to an executive search consultant within a small firm; it is quite another to trust him or her to find a new group chief executive.

Overall, clients are likely to go to the executive search firm they feel most comfortable with, which has the most appropriate range of experience and is closest to the image of the type of people they wish to recruit. It is a truism that the executive search consultant hired has a stronger influence on the person eventually put on the short list of candidates than the client. The search consultant who comes nearest to the board's idea of the chief executive they wish to hire may well be successful in winning the assignment.

The dominant issue in most searches is how well the executive search consultant understands and relates to the culture of the client. For a search firm, it is not easy with new clients to truly understand their culture and to find a range of people for a short list who would fit into that organisation in a short space of time. As ever, the acid test for search consultants is not getting the people hired, but whether those people are doing an effective job two, three or four years later. An even better test is whether, after two years, the successful candidate is promoted again or given a larger international role. Bringing a very senior candidate into a new organisation right at the top is always a very difficult matter. There may still need to be meetings and discussions between the consultant and the client even after the candidate is appointed to ensure that things are running smoothly.

HOW IS AN EXECUTIVE SEARCH CONSULTANCY INVITED INTO A COMPANY?

Clearly the firm has to be known, and a well-informed personnel director or even chief executive has often developed a number of relationships with executive search firms. The ones that study the search market even more closely will know who is particularly good at what and who has done recent searches. He or she may even know the number of consultants within a particular firm, how it has been performing, what its key issues are, how it has grown over the past year and generally what it is doing and how successfully. The executive search consultants are usually good at keeping these relationships and informing decision makers on changes in their organisation as well as general information about the search business. There is nothing more interesting to a busy chief executive or personnel director than knowing what the competition is doing, how much they are being paid and who is moving where.

The perceptive executive search consultant (a) keeps in contact with clients, both actual and prospective, and (b) is very effective at giving them this sort of information.

When the need arises to review the search firms they are using or when there is a particularly sensitive issue, then which firm is contacted is clearly a very important issue.

In a recent large international search the company in question called on five of the major search firms, and invited them all in to make a competitive pitch to decide who was going to be successful at finding them a group chief executive. However, having said that, the best way of getting new business is by referrals from satisfied clients rather than completely new assignments with completely new clients.

In summary, it is clear that the nature of headhunting in Asia is changing. It is a lot more professional than it was in the 1980s, comparable with the standards of other types of consultancies and partnership firms, and is attracting an altogether higher quality of consultants than was previously the case. In turn, clients' expectations are growing; they are more informed, more knowledgeable about the process, much more likely to adopt an open style, and want to know the key facts, expecting a high level of overall professionalism. Very few of them believe there is any magic (if ever there was) in the business and almost all of them want to understand the process and expect executive search consultants to provide that knowledge. There is now no room for the amateur in the search business.

The search market in Asia is maturing and executive search, as a service, is starting to come of age. Executive search is becoming the most effective way to recruit senior management talent into organisations. It is expensive for clients but in relation to the potential benefits which a strong appointment can produce, the fees and expenses involved can appear relatively small.

A future interesting trend may well be the 'poachers turning gamekeepers' syndrome, and vice-versa. There is some recent evidence of executive search consultants moving from major positions in search firms to become group personnel directors or even MDs of large firms or service businesses. Some executive search consultants are now becoming non-executive directors in businesses where there is no potential conflict.

The opposite side of the coin is that group personnel directors or chief executives are moving from the corporate world to join executive search firms which can offer a wholly different but very satisfying way of earning a living.

Advantages and Disadvantages of Using Executive Search to Identify and Attract Managers

Upside: Search is ideal for high-level positions or specialist roles, particularly in a tight job market, and is the most professional and objective way of solving a senior job vacancy.

Downside: It can be expensive, is for senior roles only, and success is not guaranteed, although is more likely when a good quality and appropriate firm is hired: watch out for the cowboys!

CHAPTER 3

THE ECONOMICS OF SEARCH

How does executive search compare with other methods of recruitment? It's not always the most expensive alternative. But it's a case of horses for courses, and you get what you pay for.

Price often plays a part in the decision of whether to use executive search or advertising, and it is often assumed that search is the most expensive way of solving a recruitment problem.

However, in the case of a middle-to-senior manager from around the Asian region who could be recruited by advertising or search, analysis suggests that this assumption is not necessarily correct. Depending on the salary level of the appointment, although search generally costs marginally more than do-it-yourself recruiting by advertising, using an effective and good quality search firm can save considerable staff time and therefore money, and can cut down risks in the long run.

What do users say? "Advertising can be appropriate when there is a large pool of quality candidates available", explains the group personnel director of a large American insurance group in Hong Kong.

Search can be better in a tight market for talent, when the people required are unlikely to respond to ads. We make a decision case-by-case on what method to use. We also have to take into account whether or not we need to attract people from around the region. If we use search to scour the region, clearly it has to be a firm with appropriate regional offices or associates.

As we will see in the example below, when candidates could come from all over the region, the cost-comparison between searching regionally and advertising regionally is not significant.

If it's a one country requirement, where the candidate is expected to come from the domestic market, it also depends on the country where the recruitment exercise is being carried out. "We tend to use advertising or our own networks here in Indonesia", suggests the general manager of a large American computer company in Jakarta, posted there from the United States. "Many of the search firms here don't have the necessary research skills. The local market is not geared towards search yet." However, all local markets in Asia have several well-established daily newspapers with classified sections.

In comparing executive search and other forms of recruitment, let us take a case study: the search for a marketing manager in consumer goods of a medium-sized region-wide company in the Fast Moving Consumer Goods (FMCG) sector, who would receive a salary of US$50,000–60,000. The candidates could come from a number of countries around the region. In this case, the shortage of managers requires the need to scour a wider area.

This job is at the lower end of the executive search spectrum, at the edge of a grey area between executive search and recruitment advertising. This has been chosen because middle-to-senior managers can be recruited by search or advertising. With senior managers, the options are less clear. "Senior managers can be recruited by networking, or from within, or sometimes through executive search", suggests the Chief Executive Officer (CEO) of a private banking services group in Singapore. "It's very uncommon to see advertisements for very senior positions. The sort of people in demand for these appointments do not tend to spend much time reading appointments columns."

If the would-be employers in our example had undertaken the search themselves, through placing a series of advertisements, they would be faced with several direct and indirect costs. The greatest of these would be the advertisements, which would need to be placed in a variety of newspapers throughout the region. For adequate media coverage, it would be necessary to advertise in at least one newspaper per country.

Just how much does regional advertising cost? The top rates per single column centimetre are:

South China Morning Post (Hong Kong)	HK$125	US$16.03
Straits Times (Singapore)	S$32.60	US$19.60
New Straits Times (Malaysia)	RM 27	US$10.13
Jakarta Post (Indonesia)	Rp 30,000	US$13.65
Manila Bulletin (Philippines)	P160	US $6.26
China Times (Taiwan)	NT$1,100	US$41.46
Bangkok Post (Thailand)	Bht 320	US$12.05

In this instance, the employer chose a one-eighth page ad and ran this in Hong Kong, Singapore and Taiwan only, with two insertions in each newspaper. The top rates for one-eighth page, 12 cm by 5 cm columns are:

South China Morning Post (Hong Kong)	HK$7,500	US $961.54
Straits Times (Singapore)	S$1,956	US$1,176.11
China Times (Taiwan)	NT$66,000	US$2,487.70

This would total US$4,625.35, and insertions twice would total US$9,250.70 (1994 figures).

The next heaviest indirect costs come with the time-consuming work of sifting the applications, interviewing perhaps twelve promising candidates and second interviewing at least three finalists. What does this mean in staff time? "The main reason why I use search," considers the general manager of a trading group in Malaysia, "is to avoid having to go through the screening process in-house." The administrative work in responding to possibly 100 applications – not an exaggerated number in personnel experience for a position of the salary level and status of our example – can easily take thirty hours, even though the great majority will go straight into the bin. This does not take into account any business lost whilst executives are tied up in selecting and interviewing at all stages in the procedure.

Including final negotiations to the point of signing on the dotted line, at least sixty man- and woman-hours will have been spent on tracking down this marketing manager. (How much is this costing your company? Using a blanket rate of US$100 per hour, covering executive and secretarial time, indirect costs on this selection exercise would reach US$6,000. This should really be costed in when making a decision between recruitment methods.)

Therefore, the total bill for the recruitment by advertising (excluding costs common to both forms of recruiting) would be US$9,250.70 on advertising, and potentially around US$6,000 on staff time. By comparison, how much would an executive search consultant charge, and what would the client get for his or her money?

The standard fee at this level (at 25 per cent of the salary) charged by the particular search firm in this case totalled US$15,000 and US$300 expenses, costing the employer an overall total of US$15,300. Some search firms in Asia charge lower percentages, but most of the leading professional firms would insist upon a minimum fee of around US$15,000–20,000 for a search at this level.

Comparatively, advertising could prove to be slightly cheaper and even more effective in some markets with good media facilities. However, it requires considerable staff time for processing applications which could otherwise have been channelled towards other profit-engineering tasks. Search on the other hand could be more expensive but provides a better alternative in markets without good media facilities. It can be more target-oriented as opposed to advertising which is more general in scope. Using search may help save time and provides an added value.

Contingency firms, which base fees on the successful outcome of the search, are generally cheaper than retainer firms. Some will take on assignments for only 10–15 per cent of the salary. But users are warned that you get what you pay for: "They are only interested in placing a candidate as quickly as possible," explained the general manager of a large American computer company in Jakarta, "because they don't receive the major part of their fees until this point. They rarely take the trouble to carry out reference checks. One contingency firm I used – and never again – had not developed effective techniques to screen out unsuitable candidates, and several totally inappropriate people were put forward."

Many retainer search firms see themselves more as management consultants than headhunters. They do not charge fees based on the final remuneration figure agreed with the successful candidate, arguing that this might compromise objectivity in the final stages of negotiation, which inevitably includes discussion of the salary package. They prefer to base fees upon time and difficulty of the assignment. But the majority of international search firms operating in Asia charge a standard fee of 25 per cent at this level, and 33–35 per cent at a more senior level, of the agreed notional gross remuneration of the candidate appointed, which sometimes includes a proportion of a joining bonus.

If price is not unduly significant in the choice, one of the more significant reasons for choosing search is the element of guarantee. "Many search firms guarantee to replace, without further charge, executives who leave within six months", explains the group personnel director of a large financial services group in Hong Kong. "Even those who do not offer a specific guarantee offer an implied guarantee: if they want to keep you as a client, they will be committed to the success of the assignment, even one at a relatively low-level. They know that there are plenty of other search firms around which we could go to." Also, better search firms offer such a guarantee because they know they can do the job: "A firm looking for a long-term relationship with you will be confident of finding a candidate who will 'stick', or they won't take on the job", argues a Singapore-based HR executive. "There are plenty of poorer quality firms around who promise everything but deliver nothing. You soon find out who these are and avoid them."

No such guarantee can be possible in a self-advertised recruitment exercise. For example, if the candidate recruited to this position leaves after a few months in the job, the whole expense must be repeated.

Also, the above analysis does not take account of any positive input above and beyond the scope of in-house methods which a good search consultant can provide, through their market experience and objectivity, as an adjunct to the search process. Depending upon how a company wants to make use of a search firm, and depending on the quality and experience of that search firm, they can help with background management consultancy advice on the organisation's structure, and the nature of the position the client seeks to fill; in our example, the employer admitted that "the search firm helped us to define our problems and objectives in a manner clearer than we had ever achieved before."

This sort of consulting input is less likely to be offered in a lower-level search, but reputable search firms will always 'add value' in such a way. It all depends on the extent to which the search firms starts each assignment afresh and takes the time to get to know the client. "Too many search firms just recycle their old candidates and see all companies in one sector as more or less the same", complained the Chief Executive Officer (CEO) of a computer company in Taiwan. "There is no way they can add value if this is their attitude." Also, a search firm with a small number of clients and a high level of repeat business inevitably offers more than a firm with many clients and many one-offs. "However, you must keep them on their toes", insists a major user in the financial services market in Hong Kong. "They can get lazy and offer poor quality work if they think they can get away with it."

A search consultant can also be employed to look at the existing team, to see if the best person for the job can be found on the inside, and make a comparison with those available outside in the wider market-place.

Theoretically, the search consultant can also act as a confidential middleman, keeping the client's identity and details a secret from candidates and referees alike until the appropriate agreed moment, and only then home-in on carefully selected candidates.

The company using advertising, on the other hand, must sit back and wait for the replies to the advertisements to come in. Executive search consultants argue that their methods are proactive rather than reactive. By contrast, advertising can fail to catch many ideal candidates who are not actively looking for a new appointment and do not read newspaper appointments columns, whilst bringing in a vast and random trawl including many unsuitable candidates.

In our example, the plan and search strategy was submitted within two weeks of the original briefing. It was quickly agreed with the selection committee, and a short list of four candidates was presented less than two months later. An interview programme, with candidates, the consultant and the client, was in full swing in the following two weeks and the successful candidate signed contracts less than three months from the date of the first communication between the client and the search consultant.

Employers doing their own recruiting through advertising are dependent on replies to advertisements, and cannot avoid the task of examining scores of totally unsuitable applications before meeting any suitable candidates. It is always possible that the ideal person for the job just does not exist, but advertising is not conclusive. However, a good search consultant should warn the client of this possibility at an early stage.

Overall, in making the choice between search and advertising, you must consider: How senior is the appointment? How urgent is it? Is there a large or small pool of candidates? Do we need to look all over the region or just in the domestic market? Is there a wide choice of reputable search firms to choose from? Have we had good or bad experiences of using search here? How about the 'pull' of the available newspapers? What is the extent of our in-house HR resources? Price is *not* necessarily the main issue.

PART TWO

EXECUTIVE SEARCH IN ASIA, MARKET BY MARKET

CHAPTER 4

HONG KONG

Home of International Executive Search in Asia

Hong Kong is the most mature market in Asia for search, and the headquarters of many pan-Asia search businesses. There are more search assignments given out here than elsewhere in the region, and a higher proportion of placements are due to search here than elsewhere. Although not as mature and as acceptable as in the United States or United Kingdom, search is rapidly becoming part of the business scene here, especially now after more than ten years of activity.

The substantial increase in executive search business in Hong Kong during 1992 (double the level of 1991) and in 1993 (showing a substantial increase over 1992, around 25–35 per cent) and continuing growth in 1994 indicates that this is becoming an increasingly popular option for employers, and that there has been an increase in the need for filling the sort of positions which are best suited to the use of executive search. This is especially so when people who could do the job are in short supply, are hard to find, and are unlikely to respond to ads. In

Hong Kong, this means financial services, and China-related positions.

The experiences of one prominent firm in Hong Kong are indicative of current general trends. They explained,

> Much of this increase in business for search is due to a increase in assignments fuelled by the expanding China trade. In the first half of 1993, our fee income exceeded total billings for the whole of 1992. The growth in search activity in 1994 compared with 1993 has continued, especially with the frenetic activity of the Hong Kong Stock Exchange and other stock markets around the region, and the big rise in multinationals entering and consolidating their operations in China.
>
> We undertook more than 250 assignments in 1994, and most of them were in the US$100,000 to US$300,000 per annum bracket. We've also achieved record completions: over 96 per cent of searches undertaken over the last year have been successfully filled.

Such a good record of successful completions suggests that local executives are becoming increasingly mobile and susceptible to new career opportunities; that they are becoming familiar with search as a way to change jobs; and that the clients rarely cancel searches or change their minds once an assignment has been given. Also, the search firms, especially in Hong Kong, have built up a sound degree of expertise in search, and know when a search is viable or not.

The accelerated opening up of China, more than anything else, has maintained the momentum of growth for Hong Kong search firms, and 1994 has shown an even greater emphasis on China than 1993. Most Hong Kong headhunters are spending around half their time on China-related assignments. This firm continued by saying, "The number of PRC-related assignments we have won has continued to increase over the last year. These are particularly the result of many companies building up their operations in China."

How does the firm view future prospects, especially towards 1997?

> We expect a continuing high level of hiring activity during early 1995. 1995 will be critical, and will be the point at which many returnees could emigrate again. In three years' time, at least 50 per cent of returnees will be thinking of re-emigrating. Those that do will leave gaps. Clearly, this is good news for the search business, and it also means that many young, upwardly mobile executives will enjoy accelerated promotion and increased salaries.

The *World Executive's Digest* salary survey of April 1994 saw a continuing rise in Hong Kong salaries, on average ranking third in Asia, behind Tokyo and Singapore. Hong Kong's finance executives ranked second behind Singapore in salaries in the area of sales, marketing and MIS.

NORMAN BROADBENT

Asia head office: 12th floor, Hutchison House, 10 Harcourt Road, Central, Hong Kong. Tel: 852-810-0283; Fax: 852-810-1263.

Client Comments

We need, above all, speedy and effective service, and we find Norman Broadbent has a better track record for successfully completing assignments than a number of other search firms we have tried. Many other firms see three months – rather than Norman Broadbent's average of two months or seventy days – as the norm. This can mean a lack of quality, but we haven't found this.

They are especially good in the local Hong Kong market, where they operate at quite a high level, and they can bring in the big guns from London and elsewhere when they need to. They aren't that strong in the rest of Asia, however.

Norman Broadbent does not have the global presence of Korn/Ferry, Russell Reynolds, Spencer Stuart and Egon Zehnder, and when we recommend using them to head office in the United States, it's more difficult to justify the choice, but here in Asia they do a good job for us.

Competitor Comments

Norman Broadbent is seen as well-established and of critical mass in this market, unless there is a dramatic increase in new business, when they may have to enlarge their numbers. At the moment, the number of consultants is large enough to represent a range of experience, but also small enough to allow each assignment to be discussed among everyone in the office. This is one of their strengths, compared with the more American-oriented firms.

Norman Broadbent worldwide is known for efficient and rapid searches, and for the high degree of market knowledge and range of contacts across the boards in many industries. Basically, they know people, and people on the move. Other firms place a greater emphasis on systematic research and analysis of sectors, which may be more scientific and exhaustive, but certainly adds to the time it takes to complete a search.

More assignments are handled by individual consultants at any one time at Norman Broadbent than elsewhere: their productivity is remarkable. They don't spend time on unnecessary processes.

The Firm's Specialities and Comparisons with Competitors

Domestic/external business. Samuel Wan, Managing Director of Norman Broadbent in Hong Kong, argues that the firm has more indigenous business than their main competitors – Russell Reynolds, Korn/Ferry and Spencer Stuart – yet they are still a global firm, offering the advantages of a worldwide organisation.

Generalist/specialist. However, like their rivals, they are generalists in approach, and can operate across several industries, but may be most confident in ones they have worked in themselves.

Regional offices in Asia. Norman Broadbent have few other offices in the region, not even in Tokyo, where many of their competitors have set up operations. They claim that they can serve clients and search for candidates all over the region from Hong Kong. This may be true, but it does give a strong Hong Kong-orientation to their Asian operation. Other firms, especially Egon Zehnder, Spencer Stuart and Russell Reynolds, are also prominent in Tokyo (if not in Singapore too), and this gives a wider approach to their perception of the region.

Research/contacts. The firm does not encourage research staff to approach candidates. The consultants, called 'directors', carry out their own research and sourcing. The research staff handle basic identification of candidates from directories and published sources, known as 'desk research'. These can vary from directories of people in particular sectors, magazines carrying 'people stories' and alumni lists.

Perceived differentiators. "Our main differentiators," suggests Samuel Wan, "are the high corporate levels we work in, our high success rate, and our rapid time to completion. The tradition of our firm is to publish basic information about our activities." A significant proportion (22 per cent) of Norman Broadbent's work is in finding chief executives, managing directors, divisional heads and general managers. Of their success rate, they quote 97 per cent completion, marking a rise from previous years. Of their speed of completion, the firm quotes an average seventy days. They have a high level of repeat business (at least 70 per cent).

Details About the Firm

The firm was founded in Hong Kong in 1984 as a representative office and fully established in 1986 after the aquisition of a local firm. Then it set up links with associated offices in Singapore and Taipei. The Beijing office was opened in 1993.

Number of consultants and researchers: Samuel Wan (Managing Director), Simon Swallow, Karen Fifer, Kenneth Boey, Betty Chan, Ivy Chow and Vivian Wong, and a support staff of eight, including research managers, Seema Kanwal and Catherine Tan.

The firm's operations in specific sectors of industry. These are the management positions that Norman Broadbent have most frequently filled in a recent sample:

Financial services 50%

16%   merchant banking/venture capital
43%   corporate and commercial banking
4%   treasury
37%   investment management/stockbroking

Commerce/industry 50%

38%   consumer/retailing
23%   services
11%   manufacturing
13%   telecommunications

Functions

17%   chief executives and managing directors
23%   divisional heads and general managers
23%   financial services managers
14%   marketing/sales directors and managers
7%   finance directors and controllers
10%   technical directors, MID directors
6%   human resources directors and managers

Salary and number of assignments. In 1993, the average salary per assignment increased to over US$150,000, up to US$1,000,000. The number of assignments carried out was 114 in 1993, and over 200 in 1994.

International network. Norman Broadbent in Hong Kong is wholly owned by Norman Broadbent International, part of BNB

Resources, a public listed company in the United Kingdom. Since the firm was set up, it has built up a domestic clientele, principally in Hong Kong but making use of affiliated associates in Singapore and Taiwan. Worldwide, the International Search Partnership, to which Norman Broadbent is associated, is represented in London, New York, Chicago, Barcelona/Madrid, Copenhagen, Dusseldorf, Milan, Paris, Stockholm, Sydney, Toronto and Zurich. In October 1993, Norman Broadbent became the first international search firm to open an office in Beijing. The Beijing office is a cooperative arrangement with China International Economic Consultants, a subsidiary of state-owned CITIC.

Consultants' backgrounds and expertise

Samuel Wan is a native of Hong Kong, educated at University of Hong Kong and Chinese University of Hong Kong; he has worked for Banque Nationale de Paris (BNP) in Hong Kong, and the Bank of America (BoA) covering Hong Kong, PRC, Taiwan and India; he has experience in banking, finance and retailing.

Simon Swallow is British, having lived in Asia for seventeen years; he originally qualified as a solicitor in London; has worked for Jardine Matheson in Hong Kong and has worked in Korea and Indonesia. He joined the Hutchison Group in Hong Kong; he has experience in the finance, securities and legal sectors.

Karen Fifer is Eurasian, educated at City University Business School, London; she has worked in marketing and co-ordinating exhibitions with Sun Hung Kai International Services and has search experience in consumer products, pharmaceuticals, insurance and recruitment for financial services.

Kenneth Boey is also a native of Hong Kong but received his tertiary education in the United States and Canada; he has worked for many years for the Jardines Group; and as Membership Director for the Royal Hong Kong Jockey Club; he has experience in financial control, telecommunications and China trade search assignments.

Ivy Chow is Chief Representative of the Beijing Office; she was born and raised in Hong Kong but received her tertiary education in the United States; she has experience in retailing, garment, financial services and China searches.

Changes in Supply and Demand

Samuel Wan reveals that,

in 1990, 70 per cent of our work was in financial services. Now, it's more a case of 50–50 per cent financial services and industry. Financial services have continued to grow despite fewer assignments from US banks, but the greatest difference was in the early 1990s a boom in Fast Moving Consumer Goods (FMCG) businesses, textiles, and garments, reflecting rising consumer incomes across the region, and the expansion of China-related trade. Now, in 1994, private banking, investment banking and fund management continue to be growth areas, particularly dealing in China securities. Many new China funds are being set up and China activity is increasing expedientially.

From the employee's point of view, the job market has never been better. At the moment, the local economy is very much China-driven. Roughly 40 per cent of the firm's assignments are directly or indirectly linked to China. Over the past four years, the firm's business has grown by three times, which reflects the bullish sentiment of corporations operating in Hong Kong and China. This trend is expected to continue over the next several years, but perhaps at a more variable rate.

Advice to Aspiring Executives

Simon Swallow advises that

> You should send us your résumé and we will always respond, and usually set up a meeting. There is no best way to present your résumé, but we do prefer those which start off with what the person is doing now (focussing on achievements rather than job responsibilities), and then give historical details of what they were doing before. Every week, we receive between fifty and one hundred write-ins (i.e., speculative CVs sent to us in the post), and of these between 25 and 40 per cent are useful to us, in terms of our assignments.

This is a much higher proportion than in the United States or Europe, where as many as 75 per cent or even 90 per cent of write-ins are discarded: "we receive thirty to forty write-ins per week from outside of Hong Kong, from returning Chinese, from the United States, United Kingdom and some from continental Europe. They're all looking for a job in Hong Kong." Karen Fifer emphasizes that "clients in this market are always in a hurry. They want people who are experienced, who have done it before, who can hit the ground running. Practical experience is usually more important than qualifications."

Proportion of Different Nationalities among Candidates

Simon Swallow insists that

> Our candidates can come from anywhere. Although increasingly overseas Chinese are preferred rather than expatriates, we are interested in bringing outstanding people from the United States and Europe back out to Asia, especially those who've had experience of working here before, often now in their forties. Of these coming to work in Hong Kong, 1997 certainly isn't an issue, mainly because they're unlikely to look more than three years ahead, and in any case they have American or British passports. If we place someone who hasn't been here before, we're taking a chance that it might not work out, not just with them as individuals but with their families.

Karen Fifer adds,

> But the vast majority of our candidates – over two-thirds – are Chinese by origin. Many of these are now returnees from Canada, and we have completed a number of assignments in which we have placed returnees in the last few months. Other candidates come from other parts of Asia, and especially from Australia. Many of our candidates are Chinese Americans who feel they have hit the 'glass ceiling'. They want to come back to this region so they can overcome this. Here in Hong Kong, for American Chinese, the sky's the limit, and they have many advantages, especially linguistically and culturally. Placements of Chinese who have been resident in North America or Australia is already around 10 per cent, and the proportion is growing. It has much to do with multinational and other business in China. At the moment, this is seen to be expanding strongly.

According to Sam Wan,

> Many of our candidates in Hong Kong are Chinese from other countries in the region. They can progress quickly, they don't have a language problem, and they don't have a passport problem. The rate of mobility within the region continues to increase. However, it can be hard to move if your job depends on your contacts and your reputation in one market.

Proportion of Women among Placements

"More women are appearing on short lists", reveals Karen Fifer.

> Few companies specify men or women, although some highly industrial, technical jobs rarely appeal to women and, in some countries in the region – such as Korea or Japan – it is harder for women to be successful. But there are many successful women executives in Hong Kong, especially in sales and marketing, in the garment trade, and in consumer products. There are a lot of women in banking in Asia, especially in private banking. Around one or two placements in every ten are women.

This is a much higher proportion than in the United States or Europe. "It is useful for a search firm to have at least one woman consultant in this market," Karen Fifer argues, "because we have quite a few women clients, and there is a natural empathy with a woman consultant."

Proportion of Expatriate and Local Clients

"Multinational clients account for about two-thirds of our assignments, and these are by no means mostly British", explains Sam Wan. "We have lots of US clients, and we also work for non-global companies based here, and quasi-government organisations."

Work in Other Locations across Asia

Sam Wan reveals that,

> half of our searches are beyond Hong Kong, in so far that we're looking across the region for candidates. We find we don't need to have offices in other Asian countries, although we have had experience of working effectively with our affiliates in Singapore and Taiwan, and this joint cooperation is important. Sometimes we travel to another location to interview candidates, but more often than not, they pass through Hong Kong and come to us.

"In this respect," adds Simon Swallow, "Hong Kong is an ideal base for us, located at the crossroads of Asia."

Karen Fifer explains:

> Most of our China searches are driven from Hong Kong. We work for a number of clients operating joint-ventures and wholly-owned businesses in China, and find people for them from elsewhere in the region, or elsewhere in the world. If the assignment is in southern China, these people do not necessarily live there but commute from Hong Kong.

How Important are Academic Qualifications?

"MBAs are not necessarily as important as they may seem", warns Sam Wan.

> Some employers like the idea of MBAs, but few insist on it, and most just want the person who is best able to do the job and has a good track record of experience in the field. An MBA is nice to have rather than essential in most cases, and it depends very much on the particular school or university, and the subsequent networking opportunities. Much more than academic qualifications, interpersonal skills and matching the client's culture are really significant.

Perception of the Importance of the Region

Karen Fifer insists that

> Hong Kong is more important than ever as a regional centre for Asia, at a time when Asia is more important than ever. Companies which had a representative office here are now upgrading their operation, and new companies are setting up for the first time. All the traditional reasons for coming to Hong Kong are still current, and our proximity to China is more vital than ever. The great China success stories – including Procter & Gamble and Heinz, to name only two – are encouraging others. Sourcing products within China is bigger and bigger business each year.

SPENCER STUART & ASSOCIATES (HK) LTD.

Asia head office: 4/F, St. George's Building, 2 Ice House Street, Central, Hong Kong. Tel: 852-521-8373; Fax: 852-801-5246.

Client Comments

> There are firms which will sell you a faster solution. Spencer Stuart are relatively slow and methodical, but at least you know that they've done a thorough job in scanning the market, and they have very high standards.

> Spencer Stuart have been in Asia a long time, longer and more successfully than most of the other international search firms. They are well-respected here, when there are many disreputable firms

price-cutting and trying to break into the market. We were tempted to go to one of these cheaper firms once, but not again. You get what you pay for.

Many search people move around a lot between different firms, and I've always thought that this is one of the least attractive aspects of the search business. Although there are some notable exceptions, Spencer Stuart are more likely to recruit new consultants from the business world rather than other firms. Also, it's fairly rare for staff of Spencer Stuart to leave and join competitors. I think this says something about how they see their firm.

Competitor Comments

Spencer Stuart does seem to work well as an international network, in the same way as Egon Zehnder does. The consultants are cooperative, not competitive. People in different offices seem to know each other, and draw on each other's knowledge. They strongly advocate the value of their international network; no wonder, because it does seem to work for them.

In the Spencer Stuart partnership structure, no one owns more than 1 per cent of the shares. This is in great contrast with some of the other major firms, where owner/founders still own big chunks of equity, and no one is quite sure what will happen in the future. A search consultant with equity or the chance to hold equity approaches assignments in quite a different way than those just earning a salary.

Spencer Stuart used to be seen as a firm dominated by older consultants, who may have a lot of experience but who may be out of touch with new, emerging businesses, and maybe even a bit fuddy-duddy. But they are making quite an effort to bring in more people in their thirties and forties, and develop a new generation.

The Firm's Specialities and Comparisons with Competitors

Domestic/external business. Spencer Stuart has less indigenous business than other firms, such as Norman Broadbent, for example, but more multinational work, and a particularly large proportion of clients served by Spencer Stuart globally. They are seen as especially appropriate to clients needing worldwide search capability.

Generalist/specialist. Martin Tang, Managing Director explains:

Spencer Stuart has some specialists but as a firm we are mostly generalists. We have experts whose expertise we can tap into, for product knowledge and insider insights, in our offices all over the world. We have a Japanese unit, a financial services unit, an entertainment and leisure unit, and so forth. But we have to be generalists. Most of our individual markets are not of themselves large enough to justify a collection of different specialists. Another point is that the level at which we work requires a generalist approach. Very senior jobs are not related to functional areas or specialisms. We may sometimes lose assignments to specialist boutiques, but they are mostly operating at a lower level than we are.

Regional offices in Asia. These include Tokyo and two offices in Australia, but most of the work is handled from Hong Kong, which is seen as providing a good base. Selector is seen as a possible vehicle to drive the regional network, with the future establishment of local Selector offices building up market knowledge in different localities before a search business can follow. Other firms – Russell Reynolds and Egon Zehnder – have an office in Singapore, and it may be that Spencer Stuart may re-open here when they can identify appropriate business opportunities and consultants.

Research/contacts. Research is seen as of great importance at Spencer Stuart, more so than many of their competitors. Detailed research background is provided to support all presentations to clients. Yet consultants are still responsible for much of the contacting of candidates and all the client contact.

Perceived differentiators. Martin Tang explains:

> Spencer Stuart is a strong, worldwide executive search brand, which approaches markets and sectors and clients in a highly strategic way. It's a partnership, not a corporate, and is cooperative, but not hierarchical. New partners join assimilation meetings to learn about the Spencer Stuart culture, and the firm is very serious about orientation and training.

"Spencer Stuart's origins lie in consulting rather than recruitment", emphasizes Tang. "This means that we take a problem-solving approach rather than just trying to fill vacancies."

Peter Roberts, a director of the firm suggests that,

> The size of our operation is very important as a differentiator. Some may see this as a negative, but I think our global reach is a very important feature in what we offer. We have a well-balanced network of thirty-two offices worldwide, in every major business centre, with

150 consultants, about half of whom are partners. Yet we are still a local firm. We have been here since 1976, and we are part of the fabric of Hong Kong, and arguably of this entire region. I would also add that Spencer Stuart exhibits a remarkable consistency worldwide, because our offices are wholly owned, they are not joint-ventures and we do not believe in a loose federation of individual firms.

We have also developed a comprehensive database and research expertise, locally and worldwide. We can source candidates globally, rapidly. Our database also documents the history of all assignments undertaken, locally and worldwide. So that when we make a presentation to a potential client, we are able to demonstrate evidence of our experience in that client's sector or industry, and/ or in the particular function.

Details About the Firm

Spencer Stuart was one of the first major search firms in Asia. The Hong Kong office was opened as a regional headquarters in 1976 by Paul Cheng (now Chairman of Inchcape Pacific). The firm is also well established in other offices in the region (Sydney and Melbourne from the early 1970s) and Tokyo from 1985. An office in Singapore was established, but closed in 1990. Searches in the region are conducted mostly from Hong Kong.

Number of consultants and researchers: Martin Tang (Managing Director and Regional Manager), Louise Ho, Peter Roberts, Tim Hoffman, Annie Shih, Anne Ng, and a support staff of six, including two researchers.

The firm's operations in specific sectors of industry.
These are the management positions that Spencer Stuart have most frequently filled in a recent sample:

Specialisation by industry sector

Consumer products and edibles – 26%
Financial services – 23%
Apparel – 14%
Quasi-government – 11%
Electrical and electronics – 11%
Diversified conglomerates – 8%
Industrial products and services – 7%

Specialisation by management positions

CEO/Managing Directors – 22%
COO/Regional Managers – 30%
Finance – CFO/Finance Directors – 8%
Marketing and sales – 25%
Others – 15%

Salary and number of assignments. The average salary per assignment during 1994 was over US$120,000, up to US$500,000; average fees are US$35,00–40,000 with US$30,000 as the minimum fee. Typically, the firm carries out over 120 assignments per year.

International network. Spencer Stuart is a worldwide partnership, with thirty-four offices: Amsterdam, Atlanta, Barcelona, Brussels, Buenos Aires, Chicago, Dallas, Dusseldorf, Frankfurt, Guildford, Hong Kong, Houston, London, Los Angeles, Madrid, Manchester, Melbourne, Menlo Park, Milan, Montreal, Munich, New York, Paris, Philadelphia, San Francisco, Sao Paulo, Stamford, Stuttgart, Sydney, Tokyo, Toronto, Zurich. "The Spencer Stuart network does work closely together", Martin Tang says.

> In my first three months with the firm, I met people from more than twenty offices. It's not just a name, an umbrella under which individuals work, but a cohesive whole, and totally global in reach. There is a lot of interaction between partners, and a high level of referrals between offices. Candidates can be in practically any location in the world, and we can get Spencer Stuart consultants to interview them.

About one-third of our searches in Hong Kong are referred from other offices, and we are now in a position to reciprocate.

The Hong Kong office has the closest links with other major financial and commercial centres, such as New York, Chicago, London, San Francisco and Tokyo.

Consultants' backgrounds and expertise

Martin Y. Tang, Managing Director and Regional Manager, is Chinese. A graduate of Cornell University (BSc) and MSc from the Sloan School of Management, Massachusetts Institute of Technology; he was formerly with the Bank of America (San Francisco and Taiwan), South Sea Textile Manufacturing Company (Hong Kong and Indonesia) and Techno-Ventures (HK) Ltd. He has seven years of experience in executive search.

Peter F. T. Roberts is British and a director. He graduated from the Royal Military Academy. Previously with the Redfearns Group of Companies in the packaging industry, he joined Spencer Stuart in 1992. He has nine years of experience in executive search.

Annie Shih is Chinese and a director. She joined Spencer Stuart in 1977, having graduated from the research side of the business. She has accumulated eighteen years of experience in the recruitment of senior executives, and is particularly current with key players in the consumer products sector and the China market.

Anne Ng is Chinese and a senior consultant. She graduated from the University of Hong Kong (B.A.). and was formerly with Wang Pacific and Trafalgar Housing; she has broad experience in personnel management, real estate, business development and broadcasting. She has four years of experience in executive search. Selector only.

Changes in Supply and Demand

Martin Tang notes that

> the demand for senior level executives remains strong across all industries. Asia continues to be viewed as a high growth area over the next few years, and foreign multinational companies call upon us to find people to either establish or expand their Asian offices.

Louise Ho adds,

> one trend that we have noticed in financial services recently has been the growth in emerging markets. Demand in the Indian subcontinent, Korea and certain ASEAN countries seems to have picked up in recent months.

Annie Shih continues,

> the need for senior managers in China and for people with experience in that market. We see more assignments to find executives who can cover not only China but "Greater China", i.e. China, Hong Kong and Taiwan. Demand is strong in consumer products, industrial products and in infrastructure projects.

Spencer Stuart has noticed an increasing emphasis on China searches, but there is a change in the character of these assignments.

Martin Tang explains,

> We used to be mostly looking for general managers for joint-ventures, but now we are more concerned with 'helping the Chinese spend their money', that is, searching for people to head-up retailing

operations in China. China used to be viewed only as a low-cost manufacturing base, but now China is being seen as a consumer society. This is definitely one of the most popular areas at the moment.

Annie Shih adds,

Almost every other assignment we undertake has a China component. Immediately after 4th June 1989, there was a dearth of demand for people with China experience, but now the reverse is true. People with on-the-ground experience in China are highly sought after. It's no longer such a hardship-posting, but is seen as a real opportunity.

Peter Roberts continues,

In financial services, commercial and investment banking remains important, and a particularly active area is bringing Chinese companies public on foreign stock markets, such as New York. We expect to see more work in this area, including the setting-up of representative offices for Chinese companies overseas. Our global network makes us very well placed for this.

Advice to Aspiring Executives

"Asia is still wide open to well-qualified people", argues Martin Tang. "Economies are still expanding, and there are big shortages of good managers." "There's been a big increase in Americans and Europeans sending in their résumés to us", adds Peter Roberts. "They're mostly trying to escape recession in their own countries. To be successful here, they need an ability to adapt to a different culture, and special skills and expertise, especially those which are in short supply here. They need presence and confidence."

"Of Chinese executives looking to move up, overseas qualifications and experience make a great deal of difference, especially if they are looking for a regional role", explains Annie Shih.

Overseas Chinese are the flavour of the month right now. For assignments in China, it's not always necessary to be able to speak Mandarin, although this is clearly good to have. Cantonese is good enough for many of our assignments in China, which are mostly in the Guangdong region.

When people write in and send their résumés, we are quite particular about whom we invite for interview. We don't talk to everyone by any means, although some firms here might do. We're looking for people with special talents.

Proportion of Different Nationalities among Candidates

"Most of our candidates (around 75 per cent) are Chinese, and (to re-emphasize the point) especially in demand are Chinese with experience of living overseas. But there is still a need for outstanding expatriates, even among Asian companies. There are many expatriates – Americans, Europeans, Australians – with leading Asian companies here, providing expertise they don't have in-house", reveals Martin Tang.

"We get a lot of Chinese returnees too," explains Peter Roberts, "and many fairly senior people from North America who have been restructured out of jobs, and have looked around for another job at home for a long time without success, then have read about Asia and think they will try here." "However," Martin Tang continues, "Chinese are generally preferred to expatriates by most of our clients, both multinational and local. Many Chinese are coming back from North America, and not just those who originally left to get passports", Martin Tang explains. "Chinese in America are often perceived as good technical people, but not necessarily top management material. So many return to Asia, where they are now increasingly welcome."

Proportion of Women among Placements

"There is more of a 'glass ceiling' facing women outside of Asia rather than actually in the region," Martin Tang considers, "and it's an advantage for them to be in a position where there are skills shortages, as they are more likely to get on short lists and be considered for a significant role."

"We have a majority of women consultants here in the firm in Hong Kong," adds Peter Roberts, "as women can be very good in search. Around one in eight people on our short lists are women, a much higher proportion than in Europe or the United States."

Proportion of Expatriate and Local Clients

"Our client profile is a good mix, reflecting the fact that we have been operating in this market for a long time", suggests Martin Tang. "Overall, one-third of our clients are locally-based companies, and two-thirds are multinationals. About half of our multinational clients have had experience of working with Spencer Stuart before, elsewhere in the world."

Work in Other Locations across Asia

Martin Tang reiterates the importance of China to the firm, and suggests that an office may be opened in China, if the assignments are of a sufficiently high-level quality. Yet Hong Kong is an ideal centre from which to service China's needs. "Singapore is too far away to be involved in the China boom. We find that the centre of gravity in Asia has shifted north, reflecting the importance of China. In comparison, things are relatively slow in Singapore, Malaysia and Indonesia."

Peter Roberts adds,

> Clients might ask us to look in Taiwan or Singapore if they are looking for Mandarin speakers. We need to look in more than one country for most of our assignments. We see Hong Kong as a regional centre for us, not just as a market within itself. We also look in Thailand, Malaysia and Indonesia, and some of our searches range from as far west as India and as far east as Japan. But candidates are most likely to come from the major commercial centres.

"It has become an increasing trend in executive search in Asia to be asked to look regionally, or even globally", concludes Martin Tang. "It's our job to find the best in the world, wherever they may be."

How Important are Academic Qualifications?

Martin Tang insists that,

> Qualifications are important in getting your first job or first few jobs, then your performance and achievements are more significant. For some technical assignments, specific qualifications are required, and in most cases MBAs are nice to have. But there is now such a large supply of MBAs, that they are only really worth having if they are from a top school. This has another benefit, in terms of the alumni network being useful for contacts.

Perception of the Importance of the Region

"With the increasing importance of China, Hong Kong is more and more valuable as a regional centre to companies targeting China", Martin Tang suggests. "It is an ideal centre for our operations, both search and selection, because this is where many of our clients are, both multinational and Asian."

Selection

Selector, Spencer Stuart's own selection operation, has been very successful in the United Kingdom and other parts of Europe, and was set up in Hong Kong as a regional operation (under the name Selector Pacific) at the beginning of 1992. It is run by Peter Roberts, who also undertakes mainstream executive search assignments. An additional consultant was recruited in January 1993. Selector is seen as a regional operation, and advertises regionally. "Our selection business operates at the level just below search, and is all part of selling solutions to our clients. It is a response to the dynamics of the search market."

RUSSELL REYNOLDS ASSOCIATES, INC., HONG KONG

Hong Kong office: 4107–4108 Gloucester Tower, 11 Pedder Street, Central, Hong Kong. Tel: 852-523-9123; Fax: 852-845-9044.

Client Comments

We're an American firm expanding into Asia, and we generally feel comfortable using Russell Reynolds. We see them as consistently good and reliable, and able to quickly understand our needs.

Russell Reynolds is a safe choice to make, with minimal risk. We feel that in hiring new senior people we are always taking a chance, so we don't want to take another chance with the search firm we appoint.

We like to talk to search consultants who are locals in the markets in which they operate, and we find that this is possible with Russell Reynolds. Yet, nevertheless, they have international standards, in a business where there are clearly a lot of cowboys around.

Competitor Comments

Russell Reynolds are élitist and aggressive. Often they think they know more than the client does about that client's problem, and sometimes they could be right, but they're not the choice for everyone. Some prefer a more low-key approach.

Russell Reynolds as a worldwide firm have a large number of clients, and many of these are concentrated in the financial services sector. It is sometimes thought that they have an off-limits problem, and poach from their clients in different countries.

They are known as a very blue-chip search firm with a reputation for high-quality work, well-qualified consultants, and a very smart and professional approach. They're very international, but with an American style of internationalism.

Perceived Differentiators

Raymond Tang, Managing Director, explains,

We look around the world in many of our searches, especially because of the immigration issue associated with 1997. We are selling a global product. Our network offers real value-added services for our clients.

As a firm we have invested heavily in our technological support systems, and we have developed our own software. Research is taken very seriously, and our researchers meet clients and are often promoted up to be consultants, although research is seen as a career in itself.

We don't want to be seen as American, but as an international company abiding by US laws, with international standards.

Details About the Firm

Russell Reynolds, one of the largest international search firms with twenty-four offices worldwide, originated in the United States and is owned by the firm's senior associates worldwide. Especially strong in financial services and very powerful in New York and London, the Hong Kong office was opened in 1981, followed by Singapore and Sydney in 1984, and Melbourne and Tokyo both in 1986. In 1994 the firm's 180-plus consultants conducted over 2,000 searches.

The firm's operations in specific sectors of industry.

These are the management positions that Russell Reynold's most frequently fill:

Commerce/industry

36%   Financial services
24%   Consumer products and services
30%   Technology/industrial
10%   Others

By function

40%   Chief Executive Officers/Managing Directors/General Managers
20%   Directors
40%   Managers

Salary and number of assignments. The average salary per assignment during 1994 was HK$1 million or US$130,000, and the firm completed over one hundred assignments.

Consultants' backgrounds and expertise

Raymond Tang was educated in Hong Kong and the United States, at Tufts University and Yale University School of Medicine; he worked for Johnson & Johnson in marketing management in Australia, Hong Kong and China; he has experience in executive search since 1985 in financial services, healthcare, retail and industrial products marketing in Hong Kong, China and Taiwan.

Andrew Tsui was educated at the University of Hong Kong, qualified as a Chartered Accountant with Price Waterhouse in Canada and Hong Kong; he has worked for Sun Hung Kai Securities and Irving Trust Company; he has experience in executive search since 1986, in banking, asset management, securities, properties, industry and consumer products.

Louisa (Wong) Rousseau holds a Harvard MBA, worked for Morgan Guaranty before switching to a career in retailing and textiles, both in Hong Kong and New York; she has experience in executive search since 1988, in retailing, manufacturing, sales and marketing, consumer products and healthcare.

David Waring holds a Cornell MBA, worked for Monsanto and General Electric before founding and managing two Hong Kong companies involved in marketing industrial products and services; he has experience in executive search since early 1991, in high-tech, manufacturing, industry and petrochemicals.

Addy Lee, educated in the United Kingdom at Nottingham University, worked for Dow Chemicals, Sanofi and Sandoz; he has executive search experience since 1991, in general management and sales and marketing for multinationals.

Kirsty McAlpine, educated at the University of Durham, has experience in executive search in London and Hong Kong, focussing on the financial services sector, especially investment management, broking, corporate finance and derivatives.

Theresa Wei holds a Bachelor of Science degree from the University of Oregon, began her career in executive search in 1984 when she joined Russell Reynolds Associates in Hong Kong. Her search expertise includes both the Hong Kong and Taiwan market, covering a broad range of industries including consumer, pharmaceutical, medical, financial services, insurance, computer, etc.

Dang Xin Hua holds a Bachelor degree in English Language and Literature from Hunan University (China) and a Master's degree in International Affairs from Columbia University. Born and raised in China, he specializes in assignments for multinational companies which seek to establish a presence in China. He is stationed in the Hong Kong office. Prior to joining Russell Reynolds, he worked in various fields such as insurance, telecommunications and media and journalism.

Changes in Supply and Demand

According to Ray Tang,

> China expertise, especially the ability to sell to, or buy from China, is in great demand. Ten years ago, the emphasis was on trading, now it's much more on joint-venture management and technology transfer. The people now going into China are different from the early breed of pioneers: more specific skills are needed now. People most in demand for these positions must be bi-cultural, coming from Hong Kong or China but having spent time either in schooling or employment overseas. It's a fairly new phenomenon that we are talking to people originally from China and not just from Hong Kong. This is our perspective as an international search firm: local firms may be looking at different people.

Andrew Tsui adds,

> Salaries in Hong Kong are now more stable. In the 1980s, they were moving more rapidly. The days when people were asking for – and getting – 40 per cent rises before they would consider a move are now over. But there has been a big increase in salaries for people covering China in the investment banks and securities houses. Derivatives specialists are particularly in demand.
>
> An area which has experienced a distinct decline is the computer industry, and among MIS people generally. There are no pay rises in this sector, and it is difficult for them to keep pace with inflation.

Human resource professionals who understand China practices, who are prepared to relocate into China, will command top salaries. Rather than regional human resources executives, more and more clients are looking for Greater China, i.e. Hong Kong/Taiwan/PRC expertise. Financial services needs for China are in a holding pattern after 1993 and attention is paid to Southeast Asia.

Advice to Aspiring Executives

Ray Tang advises,

> You should do a good job where you are and let people know about it. Make an impact by orienting your career and work record towards specific achievements. Make sure you'll be able to get outstanding references. The sort of questions we ask are: What has been his progression in the organisation? In the last five years, where has he moved to and what responsibilities has he gained? How well recognised is he within his industry? You must be able to position yourself well within your chosen field, and have done all you have claimed to have done.
>
> I also think that what people do outside of work is very significant. Community work and participation says a lot about a person's leadership skills. When you reach a certain seniority, you should give something back, and I don't mean just writing cheques. Our founder, Russell Reynolds, always said that the key thing is that we should aim to make a difference in business and society, and not just to make money. It needs good time management, but that's another quality we are looking for.

Russell Reynolds have prepared a booklet on writing résumés which is available on application to the firm.

Proportion of Different Nationalities among Candidates

Ray Tang reveals that,

> Eighty-five per cent of our successful candidates were Asian last year. We don't divide candidates into Americans or Chinese or whatever, but see them in terms of their cumulative experience, the languages they speak and their cultural sensitivities. As one-third of our searches relate to China, and we are bringing people in from all over to work in China, then Mandarin-speaking ability and cultural sensitivity towards China is more important to us than nationality.

Proportion of Women among Placements

"We don't keep statistics on the number of women candidates, as in the

United States law, candidates are not obliged to state sex, age, colour or religion", explains Ray Tang. "However, a third of our consultants around the world are women."

Proportion of Expatriate and Local Clients

Andrew Tsui claims that,

> We carry out more global assignments than any other firm. We are very close to our international network and share many of our searches with other offices. There are three types of business for us: global relationships with clients who use us worldwide; clients who want searches carried out in multiple locations in Asia; and clients who just use us in the local market. Very few of our searches are entirely local. Only about 25 per cent of our clients are domestic companies. Many of these are extending overseas, and find that their local networks aren't effective enough. The market for search in Asia is getting bigger all the time. Many companies are coming to us when they've never used search before, some reluctantly ('I guess we finally have to use you guys').

"We often gain searches in the United States to look in the Asian markets", adds Ray Tang. "This is partly because Russell Reynolds is a leading player in the United States, and also because of our presence in Asia, particularly our strong position in Singapore, Australia and Japan."

How Important are Academic Qualifications?

> Relevant educational qualifications are important, but in this we are influenced by what clients want. Some ask for MBAs, but this is more likely to be desirable rather than essential. Most of our candidates have been ten to fifteen years out of school, so it's less relevant. Being able to fit into a specific corporate culture is more important.

Selection

Russell Reynolds does not offer advertised selection services from any of its offices. "We have no immediate plans to introduce a selection practice," suggests Ray Tang.

KORN/FERRY INTERNATIONAL

Hong Kong office: 808 Gloucester Tower, The Landmark, Hong Kong.

Tel: 852-521-5457; Fax: 852-810-1632. (Asia regional headquarters are in Tokyo, headed by John Harlow.)

Client Comments

According to one satisfied client,

> One advantage of the size of Korn/Ferry is their knowledge of specialist sectors. They have so many consultants, that they can always field experts in a particular area. But they also work effectively as generalists.

Others are sometimes less enthusiastic.

> Korn/Ferry, like all very big headhunting firms, has a major off-limits problem, with so many clients that there's nowhere left to source candidates. And, in some of their offices, they have quite a turnover of consultants. This, as far as the user is concerned, gives rise to concern, especially about the confidentiality issue.

Competitor Comments

Competitors treat them with respect.

> Korn/Ferry has been a good training ground for consultants who subsequently start up on their own. Because of its name – it's just about the most well-known search firm in the world, as well as the largest – consultants are exposed to major clients and a wide range of assignments.

Korn/Ferry is seen as a pioneering firm in Asia, the first to open offices in Kuala Lumpur and Bangkok (the firm is already well established in Hong Kong, Singapore, Sydney, Melbourne and Tokyo). However, the firm has been seen by some as "less classy and sophisticated than Russell Reynolds, and less concerned with quality than Spencer Stuart and Egon Zehnder."

Perceived Differentiators

Korn/Ferry themselves also point to their size as an important advantage, and also emphasize their specialty practices. Additionally, they mention their team-based approach in ensuring continuity in client service, and their extensive database of 15,000 names in Hong Kong. This provides benchmarks in making proposals to clients and establishing the parameters of a search. Despite the turnover in some Korn/Ferry offices, there has been a consistency of consultants in the Hong Kong office (especially Peter Tan and Alan Choi, with the firm for more than ten years), which has helped in building up good relationships not only with foreign multinationals, but with Hong Kong businessmen.

Details About the Firm

Founded in Hong Kong in 1979, the Hong Kong office is responsible for searches in China, Taiwan, Korea and the Philippines. The Singapore office, opened in 1978, also conducts searches in Indonesia. The Tokyo office, opened more than fifteen years ago, also covers Korea.

The firm's operations in specific sectors of industry.

These are the management positions which Korn/Ferry have most frequently filled:

Commerce/industry

30%   Financial services
20%   High-technology
20%   China trade
20%   Consumer/retailing
10%   Others

By function

30%   General managers
25%   Financial services managers
20%   Marketing and sales directors and managers
15%   Merchandising
10%   Others

Worldwide, Korn/Ferry offers seventeen specialty search practices: aerospace/defence, board services (for non-executive or outside directors), consumer goods, corporate communications, education, energy, entertainment, fashion/retail, financial services, healthcare/pharmaceuticals, hospitality/leisure, information technology, insurance, non-profit, physician executives, real estate/construction, technology.

Salary and number of assignments. The average salary per assignment over the last year (1994) was US$120,000 and over. The number of assignments which the firm carries out averages 120 per year.

Consultants' backgrounds and expertise

Peter Tan is Chairman and CEO of the Hong Kong office, having joined in 1982 from Sung Hung Kai Finance in Hong Kong, after

54

working with ITT in Hong Kong and Bendix in Taiwan. An American of Chinese origin, he gained an MA from the University of Hawaii and attended the University of California at Berkeley.

Alan Choi was appointed Managing Director of the Hong Kong office in May 1993, having joined in 1981 from Burson-Marsteller, where he was responsible for business-to-business communications programmes. Previously, he worked with Trade Media, part of the Asian Sources Media Group (the owner of *World Executive's Digest*). A member of Korn/Ferry's technology practice, he attended the Hong Kong Baptist College and gained an MA from Syracuse University, New York.

Alice Humes, of Chinese origin, joined in 1984 from Coopers & Lybrand where she was involved in PRC consulting. Transferred to the Los Angeles office in 1989, she returned in 1991 and rejoined the Hong Kong team. She gained a BA from the University of Toronto, Canada.

Lynn Ogden, an American, worked in market consulting and research before joining Korn/Ferry in 1988. She was admitted into the partnership in May 1994. She gained a BA in East Asian Studies from Wesleyan University and attended a postgraduate Mandarin language programme at Beijing University, carrying out a one-year assignment in Beijing.

Lip-Ling Li, a Malaysian Chinese, joined in 1992 after sixteen years' experience in human resources, including the British Airports Authority in the United Kingdom. She holds an HND in Business Studies from West London College and a postgraduate diploma in personnel management from Middlesex Polytechnic.

Stephen Hau joined the firm as a partner in January 1994 from Heller Factoring, the Chicago-based financial services group, where he worked for ten years. Previously, he was with a Hong Kong brokerage company and the Fung Ping Fan Group. He holds a MBA and BSc from the University of Alberta.

Ami Bhatt, of Indian origin, joined in 1990 as a Research Associate and was promoted to Associate last year. She gained a BA (Hons) in Economics and Social Studies from the University of East Anglia in the United Kingdom.

Changes in Supply and Demand

The most active areas of interest now are the consumer products sector, and China-related searches. Banking and finance is returning to an active state after taking a dive in 1989–90. During 1994, more and more new financial services searches were given to the firm, especially in private banking, investment management and on the banking operations side. The garment and retail sectors continue to recruit heavily, and country manager and marketing director searches are also plentiful. "Our most active areas," explains Peter Tan, "are financial services, high-tech, merchandising and consumer products, in that order. General managers, also known as profit-centre managers, are our most important functional area."

Advice to Aspiring Executives

Alan Choi insists that

> We don't want to discourage people from writing in with their CVs but they should remember that we can't find them jobs. It depends on the assignments we are working on at any particular moment. Our time is totally given over to our clients. However, these résumés are, in most cases, added to our database. All our consultants will look at them. For your résumé to be useful, we need to know what you are doing currently in terms of the company and your position. A good cover letter will tell us what you are most interested in, especially if you are changing careers.

Proportion of Different Nationalities among Candidates

Of candidates placed by the firm, 80 per cent are Asian, and most of these are Chinese. Increasingly, they have studied and/or lived overseas. More and more, Korn/Ferry looks outside Hong Kong for candidates, but not necessarily for Western expatriates. Many of these are third world country nationals, highly sought after for their cross-cultural experience, and less expensive than expatriates. Around one in ten of shortlisted candidates are returning overseas Chinese, especially from Canada or Australia. "The first wave of emigration was in 1985–86", recalls Alan Choi. "Then they began to return in 1990. In the meantime, their peers had forged ahead. But now the returnees are catching up."

Proportion of Women among Placements

About one in ten candidates are women, also significantly more than a few years ago. They are playing more important roles in commercial banking and in consumer goods, garments and retailing. Some sectors would not have considered hiring women a few years ago. "Clients want us to find the best person for the job regardless of sex", explains Lynn Ogden.

Proportion of Expatriate and Local Clients

"Another interesting trend," remarks Alice Humes, "is that more companies are putting the head office for their international business in Asia. Many American or European companies are finding that Asia is the most important growth area of their international division, not surprisingly."

How Important are
Academic Qualifications?

Experience is more important than qualifications, but MBAs are important. MBAs were overvalued, now they are judged according to where you gained them. There is some suspicion about correspondence courses: it seems like just reading books. "About 90 per cent of our successful candidates have had a tertiary education, but an advanced degree is rarely mandatory," Alan Choi continues.

Selection

Korn/Ferry carries out selection services in the United Kingdom (under the name K. F. Associates) but does not offer this service in Asia.

CHAPTER 5

CHINA

The Greatest Recruitment Challenge in Asia

How do multinationals operating in China recruit executives for their China operations? Who are they looking for? What are the opportunities for Hong Kong Chinese, Taiwanese, Singaporeans and other Asian managers to work for foreign companies and joint-ventures in China?

Basically, employers are using any way they can to find the people they need, including executive search. They're looking for experienced managers who can run a business in China and who speak both Mandarin or *Putonghua* and English. The opportunities are almost unlimited.

SEARCH FIRMS RECRUITING FOR CHINA

The list on page 59 provides examples of various search firms recruiting for China and their key contacts:

Alfred Chown – Executive Leasing
Peter Bennett – Bennett Associates
Henry Yung – Well More Management Consultancy
Max Lummis – Executive Access
Sam Wan – Norman Broadbent
Martin Tang – Spencer Stuart
Ray Tang – Russell Reynolds
Glendon Rowell – Boyden
George Lim – Tyzack
Lynn Ogden – Korn/Ferry
Norman Wright – Egon Zehnder
Mark Jones, Elizabeth Lee – The Wright Company
Tom King – Amrop
Peter Barrett – Organisation Development Limited
Andrew Kwong – TASA
Anthony Au – Ward Howell

Many multinationals operating in China come to Hong Kong search firms – but increasingly, the Hong Kong headhunters are coming to China. Executive Leasing, a regional firm with offices also in Australia, has been operating in the People's Republic of China for several years. Bennett Associates has a relationship with recruiters on the mainland, through Well More Management Consultancy in Shanghai. Executive Access has local contacts to source candidates within China, and plans to open offices in Shanghai and Beijing, having already identified their local consultants. Among the international search firms Norman Broadbent opened an office in Beijing in the autumn of 1993; Spencer Stuart expects to be in a position to provide on-the-ground capability soon, in Shanghai; and Russell Reynolds also plan to have a liaison/research person in China. Boyden and Tyzack have informal local relationships in China to augment Hong Kong-based searches. Other major international search firms operating in Hong Kong, such as Korn/Ferry and Egon Zehnder, are also active in China. The Wright Company has a Beijing Office.

To a lesser extent, such multinationals also approach search firms in Taiwan and Singapore; but many of the search firms there are affiliated to international firms also operating in Hong Kong. Although they may be brought in to help with a search, many companies recruiting for China approach Hong Kong consultants first.

China-based Searches on the Rise

Search firms in the China trade have noticed a dramatic increase in the proportion of China-based searches over the last eighteen months to two years. Executive Access, over the last year, has become one of the most prominent Hong Kong firms in China executive search. Max Lummis comments:

> Eighteen months ago, under 15 per cent of our assignments were China-related searches. Today 30 per cent, maybe 40 per cent, of our work is hiring people for China. Looking at the broadest definition, at jobs involving some travel to China, the proportion could be as high as more than 50 per cent. We have completed over fifty placements in China over the last year.

Martin Tang of Spencer Stuart comments that all regional jobs searched out of Hong Kong have a China element. He finds that 10–20 per cent of his firm's assignments are for jobs based in China, and over half the jobs searched involve working and travelling in China on a regular basis. Sam Wan of Norman Broadbent, with around 40 per cent of his firm's work related to China, finds that "it's hard to differentiate China searches from non-China searches as nearly every position has an element of China responsibility now."

How the Search Firms Handle China Assignments

Most of the international search firms are exclusively interested in placing overseas Chinese or ethnic Chinese living elsewhere in Asia into China. They would visit China to meet clients and discuss the nature of the position to be searched, but would not actually search for candidates in China. Sam Wan of Norman Broadbent talks to Hong Kong candidates in Hong Kong, while his colleague Ivy Chow, based in Beijing, talks to clients on the ground, and explains what it is like to live and work in China for overseas Chinese candidates. She advises clients on local tax issues, on how to find office space, offering a service to clients of Norman Broadbent offices all over the world who are interested in China.

Martin Tang of Spencer Stuart interviews executives working in China when they come on rest and recreation trips to Hong Kong and hunts overseas Chinese all over the world: "you can't get these people from advertisements. They're hard to find. You need an international search facility, and you have to be creative." Ray Tang of Russell Reynolds also carries out a lot of recruiting for China out of Hong Kong.

> China-based executives are always travelling in and out of China, very often to Hong Kong. Not many China executives are permanently-based in China. If we do want to visit China to meet

these people, it's now getting easier. IDD telephones are more widespread, big multinational communities are being formed in China, especially in Shanghai, and you can fly up and meet a lot of people in a short time.

Executive Access has an extensive research function tracking companies and executives, developing a database; they claim this as one of their key differentiators.

Having an office in China is seen by clients of these search firms as an asset, but not essential, unless they're involved in searching for PRC nationals on the ground. And China is such a large, diverse place, that arguably no one can claim to be in China if they have only one office.

RECRUITMENT OPTIONS

It all depends on whether the client wants to hire PRC nationals, or is looking to appoint an overseas Chinese. The former is usually seen as most attractive, with on-the-spot knowledge and cultural and linguistic sensitivities. Overseas Chinese, from Hong Kong, Taiwan, Singapore and elsewhere in Asia, as well as from North America and Europe, are more expensive and not always successful. But experienced PRC nationals are in short supply.

As Peter Bennett of Bennett/Well More points out

There's a growing demand for recruitment services for China-based positions, both in and out of China, and especially in China. Multinationals should use their own means and methods first and only when these are exhausted should they come to consultants.

What are the alternatives in recruiting executives? You can try networking through your existing staff, but this can lead to nepotism; you can use official channels, i.e. FESCO, but they don't always give you what you want (although they are becoming more adept at matching skills to job requirements); and you can advertise in local or national newspapers, but there are a number of problems with this: you can get flooded with irrelevant applications, and it is impossible to predict exactly when your advertisement is going to appear, so if timing is crucial, this method is unlikely to work satisfactorily. The annual job fair can be total chaos: last year, in Shanghai, more than five times the expected number of candidates turned up, and employers found these people to be mostly inappropriate. "You may as well pin a notice to a tree and wait for people to walk in!" comments Bennett.

Bennett's responsibility in China searches is to look for overseas Chinese and the occasional Western expatriate; his associate Henry Yung and his team in Shanghai looks for local managers and technicians attracted to work in multinational companies. Bennett carries out interviews to check the suitability of the PRC nationals for multinational clients' requirements. Bennett/Well More is one of the few executive search firms offering capability to search for both overseas Chinese and PRC nationals (with Executive Leasing, of which more later).

Targets of Searches

Who are the headhunters looking for? It depends on the industry and the level. According to Ray Tang of Russell Reynolds in Hong Kong,

> China-related assignments fall into four categories. At the top are the Greater China heads, covering Hong Kong, China and Taiwan. Next would be the area heads, covering Hong Kong and China or Hong Kong and Taiwan. Then there would be the country managers and heads of joint-ventures. Finally, we would also look for direct reports, executives heading up functions such as sales and marketing, technical services, and human resources, who report to the country manager.

Russell Reynolds works primarily at these levels, as do the other international firms; positions below these are unlikely to justify headhunters' fees.

For the highest-level jobs (heading-up Greater China operations covering Hong Kong, China and Taiwan), the person would be most likely to come from Hong Kong, having had the most exposure to international management. He or she could also come from Taiwan or Singapore (capitalising on the language similarities) or could be a Western expatriate with Mandarin capability and China experience. "It would be unusual to have a Greater China director running Hong Kong out of Beijing or Shanghai, but it's an increasingly popular strategy to run China out of China", comments Ray Tang.

Area heads are also likely to be overseas Chinese. "The first two layers of management tend to be filled by expatriates – either ethnic Chinese or Westerners – but PRC nationals are coming up, especially with moves generally to localise these positions as far as possible", adds Martin Tang of Spencer Stuart. Country managers and functional heads reporting to them are also predominantly overseas Chinese, but many multinationals are keen to develop PRC managers to fill these slots in the future.

Bringing Back Overseas Chinese

At the moment, according to Peter Bennett,

> there are relatively few successful international executives in China,

so generally we need to bring in overseas Chinese. We have to find Chinese who are willing to return, identifying those who may not have immediate experience but have technical skills, language capability, and an affinity for China, who could step into these roles.

Max Lummis of Executive Access agrees. "Our clients want PRC nationals but it's rare to find locals with the experience they need. But they'll consider overseas Chinese, especially mainland people returning from studying in North America and Europe."

This doesn't always work, however. Ray Tang of Russell Reynolds warns,

> Overseas Chinese who left China during or after 4th June 1989 may not fit China today. They have connections but these may not be current, and need to be tested. Many of them are not prepared to go back immediately, and want the security of another passport or green card.

Peter Bennett points out that many overseas Chinese have failed in China, because they were not prepared for the environment, and wouldn't adjust, or they had a superior attitude to the mainlanders, and couldn't get on with people.

Yet, "ironically, many returnees (Hong Kong Chinese who left to get Canadian or Australian passports before 1997) are successfully taking up jobs in China," points out Sam Wan, especially if they've found re-entry into Hong Kong difficult, "we receive thirty to forty write-ins per week from outside of Hong Kong, from returning Chinese, from the United States, United Kingdom and some from continental Europe. They're all looking for a job in Hong Kong." "Others who have succeeded in frontier economies, who've worked in India, Indonesia, Africa, the Middle East and provincial Philippines, can do well in China", considers Peter Bennett. "They must have interest in the Chinese culture and language, and the recruiter must know how to identify this. This can include ethnic Chinese from anywhere in the world, and a small number of Westerners, perhaps only 10–15 per cent of those I place for clients."

Hong Kong Chinese and Taiwanese

The vast majority of these search firms' candidates are Hong Kong Chinese, and there are good reasons for this. According to Sam Wan of Norman Broadbent,

> If it's a manufacturing assignment in China, it could be that a Taiwanese executive may be selected; if it's a service-related

assignment, it's more likely to be a Hong Kong Chinese. Most of our candidates are Chinese expatriates; there are relatively few Westerners.

Other things being equal, we prefer to put in Hong Kong Chinese into jobs in China. Logistically it's easier as Hong Kong Chinese are more mobile. Hong Kong Chinese are on higher pay levels than Taiwanese, and expect a premium of 30–40 per cent to move to China, whereas Taiwanese may be on a lower salary level but would expect a 100 per cent premium to move to China. We also have to cope with the relative immobility of Taiwanese. If we are approaching a Taiwanese to go to China, his parents will object and put pressure on him. Taiwanese parents don't want their children to go overseas and, even though we're talking about executives in the late 30s and 40s, they still take a lot of notice of their parents. Meanwhile, getting into China is seen as more and more attractive to Hong Kong Chinese, mindful of their future. You can now attract better and better quality of people to go to China. Even Hong Kong-based international bankers will consider a career move to China. Thus, the majority of candidates are Hong Kong Chinese.

So, the headhunters are primarily looking for overseas Chinese with China expertise and experience. They may be elsewhere in the region or in the world, or they may already be in China, working for their client's competitors. "Our targets include people already working in joint-ventures in China, who know what they're getting into", reveals Ray Tang. "There's some recycling of executives already in China. The next best thing is someone who travels up to China regularly."

AN IDEAL CANDIDATE

According to Max Lummis, an ideal candidate for an executive position in China is a graduate from a top school in China. He or she has worked for a multinational for five to six years, has received intensive training overseas, and is willing to be mobile within China. Excellent language skills in Mandarin and English are essential. Such people can be PRC nationals but, having been out of the country for some time, they will require expatriate packages.

Martin Tang sees an ideal candidate for a China job in a wider perspective: he or she doesn't have to have been educated in mainland China, as long as prior China experience has been gained, and the candidate has the language ability and necessary technical skills and industry experience. Of considerable importance to multinationals is an awareness of business ethics and integrity: "they want someone they can trust", insists Tang. Employers also want someone who is not afraid to roll up their sleeves and get on with the job. "They won't have that many troops to command, so they will have to do all the jobs", Tang continues. "They need to know how to get round the system, and can't take things for granted."

Choice Between Old or Young Executives

China can be a good opportunity for older executives, for two reasons. Peter Bennett suggests that,

> Some younger expatriates will ask, what next after China? So it can be a good idea to send in older people, end of career expatriates, who are happy to give their expertise before retirement. This avoids the reluctance of younger executives who may see especially remote China postings as a backwater, or wonder how their experience in China can help them in the future.

Secondly, Martin Tang warns of the lack of facilities for young families in China.

> We are looking for people at a certain stage in their career when they don't need access to good schools. Beijing is relatively good as it has a big international community, but otherwise this is difficult. It's best if our executives for China are younger, or older, or without children.

JOB OPPORTUNITIES IN CHINA

Practically all job functions are in demand in China. Sam Wan reveals,

> We are looking for GMs, chief representatives, human resources directors, financial controllers, sales and marketing directors, technical managers, engineering and project managers, and managers with expertise in telecommunications, power plants, retailing, and setting-up and running manufacturing facilities. We have clients in manufacturing, high-tech, chemicals, and FMCG looking for executives for placements in China.

Peter Bennett has China-based clients in consumer goods, manufacturing, marketing, food, beverages, personal care products, and banking. Max Lummis has clients in FMCG, industrial and capital goods, banking and finance, telecommunications and other high-tech areas. Martin Tang's clients are in consumer goods, manufacturing and, to a lesser extent, banking.

Salaries

Salary levels for China executives – and here we're talking only about Chinese or Western expatriates – are on a par with the rest of Asia, perhaps even higher. According to Ray Tang,

> salary levels for senior, internationally-qualified people going to China are quite high, especially including the hardship allowance. A country manager or function head may be paid around US$100,000 to US$250,000 per annum cash with a premium of 25–40 per cent hardship allowance, plus house, plus travel home, which works out at a relatively high cost to the company.

Hardship allowances are usually 20 per cent for Shanghai and Beijing, and 25–30 per cent for other cities, adds Sam Wan. Employers have to give people housing in Shanghai and Beijing. "At the senior level, housing, rest and recreation trips out of China, and hardship allowances are paid," agrees Martin Tang, "although some can commute to Southern China, especially to Shenzhen."

People's Republic of China nationals are not yet able to command the salaries earned by expatriates, but the gap is gradually closing.

Peter Bennett comments,

> Managers at departmental level in the People's Republic of China earn from RMB 1,500–3,000 a month, with substantial allowances for housing, holidays and travel. In US dollar terms, PRC managers are earning around US$5,000–6,000 per annum including benefits. However, some are demanding huge pay rises, asking for salaries of up to US$30,000 per annum, and some multinationals are starting to pay this. These rises are too much, too soon, and are making life difficult for multinational investors in China.

Yet Max Lummis of China Access points to salaries of nearly RMB 200,000 per year (or around US$25,000) being earned by PRC nationals with multinationals, especially as financial controllers, and in assistant general manager positions in large foreign enterprises in consumer or capital goods.

PROBLEMS OF RECRUITING IN CHINA

Peter Bennett points to the problems of finding PRC nationals.

> Basically, there is no such thing as executive search in China. There are few executives, and making telephone calls is not easy. Until you have a much larger presence of foreign multinationals, who

have trained up local executives, and telephone companies, such as AT&T, this situation will continue.

No one has a databank of PRC nationals with management experience, claims Bennett, and

it takes more time to find them, and assess their experience. Hong Kong people are free to make decisions and move when they want to, but People's Republic of China people aren't, and relatively few people speak English. Searches take much longer: at least six weeks, or two months.

Fees Charged by Search Firms

These firms are mostly in the market for expatriates coming into China, executives who can justify the fees charged. The searches nearly always take longer and can be logistically complex, so firms often charge a flat fixed fee, based on the time the search is expected to take and the number of searches commissioned by the client. Would-be users of headhunting services are advised to approach a number of firms to compare China experience and familiarity with the industry.

Peter Bennett explains that the recruitment of PRC nationals is carried out through his firm's local operation, also charging fixed fees. He advises,

When you use consultants in China, you should buy their time, not the results. If you try to buy on results only, you're liable to get nepotism, and inappropriate people. And searching in China requires PRC capability. Also, a Hong Kong-based consultant searching in China costs too much. The job is time-consuming because there are not enough telephones, and information is not easily available. If you're looking for PRC nationals, you need a local consultant to whom you can pay local prices.

LEASING EXECUTIVES FOR CHINA

Alfred Chown, of Executive Leasing, puts leased executives into China, offering a more viable solution than full-time executives for many employers. Chown explains:

to get a new manufacturing operation up and running in China, or to implement new production or Quality Assurance procedures in China, using a leased executive has many advantages. In China, we lease plant engineers, purchasing and material control managers, engineering managers and quality assurance managers. The leased executive can train existing personnel, so that a less experienced executive can take over when the assignment is over.

We already have contract personnel in China who are Hong Kong expatriates, who live there during weekdays coming back home at weekends. They can get paid HK$14,000 a week, with accommodation and allowances on top; the average would be around HK$56,000 a month.

Executive Leasing has set up a representative office in China, reflecting the fact that assignments in China continue to increase. All the clients are Hong Kong-based, in engineering, textiles, semi-conductors and the food industry.

Chown's firm is frequently retained to search for management talent in China on behalf of Western firms. Often, a joint-venture insists on finding PRC personnel, rather than Hong Kong Chinese.

But most of the executives in China have limited management experience in the Western sense, but we have been able to find some good people from research institutes, who tend to have Western knowledge. They prefer to work for a short period rather than permanently. Also, we recruit people from competitor companies in the same industry, but it's hard to find them, and if these are Chinese companies, it's a hard job to get them out of their unit. They may want to join a joint-venture, but usually their company wants to keep them. It can take two months to get someone out of their unit, and often our client has to pay compensation to the unit to be able to do this, although some people do just walk out.

Executive leasing suits PRC nationals too. A Chinese manager can leave his unit for a relatively short time, but if he leaves it permanently, he can lose his housing allocation and all the benefits of working for the unit. One way to avoid this is for both husband and wife to work, with the husband in the joint-venture, and the wife in the state system for purposes of security and for housing.

All appointments in China are supposed to be made through FESCO, who holds the sole rights to lease out people from state units to joint-ventures, but this is now being challenged.

Chown explains,

We now tell people to report to FESCO before joining our client. This should be just rubber-stamping but FESCO is arguably interfering too much. The economy of China is now outstripping China's economic structures. With its mandate from the Government, FESCO is still important, and this is locking up the mobility of labour. We still have to launder appointments through FESCO, who see companies like Executive Leasing as a direct threat.

CHAPTER 6
TAIWAN

More Mobility, Especially with the China Connection

Salaries are rising as executives move more frequently in the buoyant Taiwan economy. But with most employers looking for Taiwanese with global expertise – especially to enter China – there's not much scope for non-Chinese here.

Executive search in Taiwan is becoming more widespread, as job mobility is on the rise; as the need for managers exceeds demand and the shortage of experienced global managers becomes Taiwan's biggest corporate problem; and whilst deregulation continues, fuelling Taiwan's growth, currently at 10–15 per cent per year. There are around thirty search firms in Taiwan, operating at different levels. Yet branded search firms – such as Korn/Ferry, Russell Reynolds and Spencer Stuart, for example – have not established a presence on the ground here, although they do conduct searches for clients in Taiwan out of Hong Kong. The market is dominated by local firms, although some of the most successful here are affiliates of overseas firms. The advertised search market is also significant, although advertising rates in Taiwan newspapers are so costly that search is a viable alternative.

As in the case of Hong Kong and – to a greater extent – Singapore, most search firms are generally working on behalf of multinational clients, although many local companies expanding overseas are using search too. If you're looking to hire executives for Taiwan, the firms listed here are most active and highly-regarded by employers. If you are a Taiwanese looking to change jobs, these are the firms to network among. But if you are a Western or other non-Chinese expatriate, you may find – unless you are a fluent Mandarin-speaker – that executive openings in Taiwan are thin on the ground.

The nature of the recruitment scene in Taiwan is changing as the economy is making the transition from being totally export-geared, to an increasing interest in imports (reflecting the growing consumer demand of twenty million people) and being more service-than manufacturing-oriented since currency controls were lifted in 1987. Together with the emergence of the Taiwanese 'Chuppies' [Chinese yuppies] is a more outward-looking mentality and, in the short- and medium-term, China-related positions are driving the market. Multinationals are using Taiwanese to enter China, and Taiwanese executives are expected to play a big role in China over the next twenty years. Being Mandarin-speaking, they're often seen as more acceptable than Hong Kong Chinese. US companies in particular are looking to the Taiwanese to penetrate China, due to the traditionally strong relationship between the two countries and influence of the United States in creating Taiwanese manufacturing and early managerial groups.

EXECUTIVE SEARCH FIRMS IN TAIWAN

International Firms

Amrop (Dr Lo & Associates)
Boyden
Dynatech (link with Norman Broadbent in Hong Kong)
TAO
Traub, Au & Associates (member of Ward Howell International Group)

Local Firms

Columbia
L&M Consulting
Resources Management Consultants
SGV Soong

Names of Outstanding Consultants

Of the international firms, Dr Vincent Lo of Amrop; Georgiana Kolenaty of Boyden; Manuel (Manny) Lopez of Dynatech; Eric Dieny and Michelle Kung, Research Manager, of TAO; Christopher Traub and Bernard Wathen of Traub, Au & Associates.

Of the local firms, Robert Yen, Human Resources Vice President of Columbia; Rosemary Yang, General Manager of L&M Consulting; Nelson Chen, Managing Director, Resources Management Consultants; Mrs Hsieh of SGV Soong.

Sectors of Industry in which Firms Specialise

Traub and Wathen specialise more by function than industry. "We recruit senior-level general managers and regional managers, especially in banking, financial services, IT, computers, capital machinery, and consumer products", they observe. They point to current shortages in marketing, advertising, PR and especially in financial services. Lo mentions these skills in short supply: training, consulting, recruiting, and banking. Sixty per cent of Lo's business is in consumer goods and pharmaceuticals. Fifteen to twenty per cent of his searches are for HR managers, followed by general managers, and managers in finance, operations, then sales and marketing. The last named is most in demand in Taiwan.

As Lo comments

> Marketing people move around more than anyone else, even financial executives or managers in advertising companies. The computer industry is down, but semiconductors are still growing. The China connection is very important. The Taiwanese are culturally very close to the Chinese in the People's Republic of China.

Kolenaty of Boyden considers that there are not so many general manager searches as there used to be, and Lopez of Dynatech sees financial services as particularly strong now. "Consumer products fluctuate, but are good now, with a lot of hiring going on."

Average Salary per Assignment

Salary levels are high in Taiwan. The Annual Compensation Survey found in the April 1994 issue of the *World Executive's Digest,* revealed that middle and junior managers (those generally recruited through selection advertising more than search) in Taiwan earned the highest gross salaries in the region after Tokyo and Singapore. Taiwan is the third most highly paid location for HR managers, and Taiwanese executives in finance, sales and marketing and engineering are also doing particularly well in terms of salary, only slightly behind Hong Kong.

Traub refers to average salaries of his placements of US$90,000, rising disproportionately to the labour force. Lo points out that "annual salary increases of 10 per cent across the board over the last ten years have been a feature of Taiwan." The rate has been even higher in marketing, whilst inflation is lower than 3 per cent. The biggest salaries, according to Lo, are paid in marketing and banking. The highest salaries he headhunts for would be NT$5 million (around US$200,000, and the lowest NT$1 million (around US$40,000). Boyden's average fee was US$18,000–25,000 last year, when 80 per cent of their searches were based on fees of 33 per cent. Salaries of Boyden's placements range from NT$1.4 million to NT$2.5 million. Lopez quotes a salary range of NT$1 million – 4 million, commenting that "compensation is low relative to Hong Kong."

Advice to Aspiring Executives

Traub reveals that

> Many people want to work in Taiwan from the rest of the region, as they are attracted by the high salaries and growing economy. We get lots of résumés from across Asia. But I would suggest, don't send your résumé all over the place. There are lots of firms springing up here, there are low barriers to entry, and not all firms are of high quality.

Lo warns prospective candidates against being too pushy, or thinking that their first meeting with a headhunter is a job interview: "I would meet candidates as a friend first, before pursuing specific job ideas." Boyden receives ten to fifteen write-ins a day, probably more than other firms, as this is the largest search firm in Taiwan and has been around the longest. Lopez welcomes résumés by post, as all search consultants in Taiwan agree that recruitment research is very difficult here; there are not even press announcements of new appointments. People in multinationals tend to be more mobile, and people in local companies are harder to move, even though in Taiwan's tight executive job market they could expect to increase their salaries and promotion prospects this way. "Some executives in local companies think, 'is this a guy sent by my boss to test my loyalty?' when I call them", reveals Lopez. "It's also not yet well known among multinationals that Taiwanese are good for China, and when they do approach Taiwanese, it's not always easy to get them to move." Traditionally, there's not the job-hopping tendency here as in Hong Kong, but people are more mobile than in Japan. In Taiwan, it's less a case of giving advice to executives wanted to be headhunted (unless they're non-Taiwanese) than pursuading Taiwanese that they *should* be headhunted.

How Important are Academic Qualifications?

"You don't have to be educated abroad, but spending ten to fifteen years in a multinational is seen as highly desirable", comments Wathen. He adds,

> But at the same time, you need local hands-on experience, preferably with contacts in mainland China. Executives are becoming more sophisticated about career planning, fuelled by overseas education, which is seen as a prerequisite for joining a multinational.

In going to overseas university, ties between Taiwan and the United States are especially strong. European schools are not that well known in Taiwan. If you want to be in banking, financial services or marketing for a multinational, you must have an MBA, but this is less mandatory for trading houses. "There's a need for Taiwanese overseas to return to Taiwan" continues Wathen, "as we especially need strong English skills, which are not so good here, and bi-culturalism is needed most of all." Lo confirms that overseas study is useful for working in multinationals, mainly because it means better English skills. He also points to the high proportion of PhDs and higher degrees in Taiwan. Lopez sees financial services as being one of the most important sources of demand for MBAs: "the new banks coming in over the last few years – the number of banks rose from two to thirty-three almost overnight – captured many Taiwanese MBAs."

Proportion of Expatriate and Local Clients

Search consultants with international search firms in Taiwan feel that among multinationals, search in Taiwan is widely accepted, in both middle and senior management, but this is not the case among local companies; "they don't want to pay for recruitment services, and they don't want to pay retainers", one commented. As a result, 95 per cent of their work is for global clients. "Slowly, Taiwanese companies are using search", explains another.

> They were started by family members but rising labour costs are forcing them to be more competitive, so there's a need for professional managers. They need to be educated about using

search. This process is encouraged when multinationals make partnerships with local companies.

Proportion of Women among Placements

Wathen notes that around 10 per cent of his firm's placements are women. "Taiwan is male-dominated, but women are increasingly taking the decision to have a career." Lo sees many women candidates, and thinks there is little discrimination: "there are as many as 30 per cent women candidates for middle management jobs." Women's chances in the job market are helped by the fact that men have to do two years military service.

Looking towards Other Countries as Sources of Candidates

Although managers from around the region – as well as Western expatriates – want to work in Taiwan, most clients want Taiwanese. Traub reveals that 99 per cent of his placements are senior level Chinese. There are only about 20,000 expatriates in Taiwan. Lo's candidates are all Taiwanese.

Perceived Competitive Differentiators of Firms

The length of time in the market is of considerable importance in Taiwan, given the lack of published candidate information sources. Boyden is seen as the pioneer of search here: when they started up in Taiwan in 1982 at the initiative of the Hong Kong office, with Investec (a market research and HR consultancy, founded in 1979) as licence-holder, "everything was on contingency, and nobody wanted to pay. HR people thought they could find executives on their own," explains Kolenaty, who first came to Taiwan in 1976 working in public relations (PR) for the Ritz. "We used to run ads to develop our database. It's now over 6,000, all interviewed by us." But by 1985, the search business started to click. There was more demand for quality search services, as many European and US companies arrived in Taiwan, and they found that ads were no longer bringing in good enough people. "1986–90 were very good years", Kolenaty continues. "1989–90 saw the lifting of the ban on imported consumer goods, and lots of foreign consumer goods companies wanted marketing managers. You won't see anything like the late 1980s again. This was a big boom time."

Traub, Au & Associates claim to be one of the only totally retained search firms in Taiwan. "Many others invoice the last fee tranch when the contract is signed and when the successful candidate starts work", Traub suggests. He sees Boyden as one of the most active in town: "they had a head start in getting multinational clients through being first in the market."

In explaining the absence of more search firms on the ground, Traub points to the serious restrictions on headhunters setting up here, due to controls imposed by the Council of Labor Affairs.

> It's now more difficult than before, yet now you really need a search firm on the ground to be effective. I've hired 200 plus people for over forty corporations, mostly blue-chip ones. Clients are having frequent management changes now, so there's lots of work. The branded search firms are serving some big clients but are not able to develop new business locally through not being here. They would need a long start-up, as it took me five years to get to the stage of around forty assignments a year, and some feel that salaries are too low to attract branded search firms. In 1993, actual numbers were down but revenues have increased as the searches are at a higher level. This trend has continued in 1994.

Vincent Lo started his search business in Taiwan in June 1989. Headhunted by Spencer Stuart – who also attracted him to the search business – he concentrates on a small range of clients with whom he has a close relationship. "I have five to ten assignments on at any one time. My biggest difficulty is finding candidates." Lo has four specialisms – sales and marketing, general managers, industry, finance – while other firms are more generalist.

Manny Lopez is a Filipino Chinese with long experience in Taiwan. He entered the search business with Columbia and then founded Dynatech, at the time when Boyden had just set up shop. Lopez, who represents Norman Broadbent (with a representative in Singapore and an office in Hong Kong) in Taiwan, is a generalist operator, completing about fifty searches per year.

The search market in Taiwan has been estimated as generating around NT$80million (US$3million) in fees, with Boyden at around NT$30million (US$1.2million); Traub at around NT$15million, and Lo at around NT$20million. Korn/Ferry, Russell Reynolds and Spencer Stuart claim around NT$10million a year. Ranjan Marwah's firm, Executive Access, is also working in Taiwan out of Hong Kong.

CLIENT COMMENTS

A user in the consumer product section points out that,

> Clients buy on price a lot in Taiwan. Boyden charge 33 per cent of

the salary for management jobs, and 25 per cent for lower-level jobs. They find that many competitor search firms underbid them. But really, it's worth paying extra for a more professional job, and users are beginning to get the message.

A frequent user in financial services reveals,

> Some of the better firms enjoy a lot of repeat business with existing clients. Both Traub and Lo – and probably Lopez – have about 70 per cent. Traub apparently did thirteen jobs for one client last year. His searches take around six weeks, although fast ones only four. This is quite rapid, compared with Western markets especially. Some clients want to see candidates in ten days and won't give one firm exclusivity. The better search firms won't accept this.
>
> There are low barriers to entry for search firms here, and a lot of dubious operators. Many call themselves executive search firms, but the word 'headhunter' is more well known. There are many poor quality start-up firms here calling themselves executive search firms but not operating at the senior management level, so it can be hard for clients to differentiate. It's best to choose a member of an international search group, or ask other users for referrals.

ADVERTISED RECRUITMENT/ SELECTION IN THIS MARKET

"Lower level search has mushroomed recently", reveals Lo. "There are now at least twenty to thirty firms in contingency work and advertised recruitment. Middle managers are poorly trained, and there's an acute shortage of them here." Advertisements are one way of reaching them, but clients have become fairly dissatisfied with the results. Mobility among this group in particular is increasing, accounting for the rise in salaries among middle to junior managers.

Boyden sometimes advertise, "but we only run ads when it's a wide ranging search with a big population of potential candidates", reveals Kolenaty. "We might also use ads for a multiple search, for a lot of people to join a company at once. For example, when we're asked to help in the setting up of a whole plant for a foreign company, we'd advertise."

One large semiconductor company complained that,

> Advertising is very expensive in this market. It's actually more expensive than anywhere else in Asia. Per single column centimetre in *The China Times*, we have to pay over US$40, four times the cost of advertising in the *New Straits Times* in Malaysia, twice as much

as the *Straits Times* in Singapore, and nearly three times as much as *The South China Morning Post* in Hong Kong. This makes users think twice about advertising, but often there's little alternative (1993 figures).

However, the CPA firms established recruitment advertising services during the late 1970s and early 1980s, and this business has also attracted a large number of local firms, of which three are listed below. There are many more, but few which are enthusiastically recommended by users. Job hunters can try sending their résumés here too but, in Taiwan, given the scarcity of candidates and difficulties in finding them, it may be better to target the search firms in the first instance.

SELECTION
International Firms

Ecco Services (associated with Hong Kong-based Ecco Services)
Persona Taiwan (Japanese firm)
Excalibur (PA affiliate) does some search work
Staff Service (Japanese firm)
Price Waterhouse
KPMG Peat Marwick

Local Firms

Personnel Express Co., Ltd.
Sung Yee
Manpower, Inc.

CHAPTER 7

SINGAPORE

Still a Land of Opportunity

If you are looking to hire executives or if you are in the market for a new job in Singapore, there's an active search market here. But it has yet to penetrate local companies remaining goussed on multinationals.

After Hong Kong, the Lion City is the most well-developed headhunting market in Asia. In terms of both executive search and selection, Singapore has attracted a wide range of international firms, and several local firms have emerged.

However, the vast majority of their assignments (especially executive search) are on behalf of multinational clients rather than local Singaporean companies. So, if your task is to recruit executives for your multinational branch, then using executive search is common practice, and here we list details of the most active firms in the market-place. If you haven't used executive search before, the information here will help you decide if it could be appropriate.

But, if you're looking for a new job in Singapore (either as a

Singaporean or as an expatriate) and you would particularly like to work in a multinational, send your résumé to the executive search firms, particularly those with international networks. Send it to the selection firms as well, as we indicate below, they also access their databases for clients to replace or augment the need to advertise. They cannot promise you a job as the clients of both search and selection firms are employers rather than job seekers, but being on their databases is a must for the upwardly mobile. Between them, they fill around a thousand executive positions a year, and that's only the search firms. With an increasingly tight market for Singaporean executives, employers are looking outside, to Malaysia, Indonesia, the Philippines and elsewhere, to fill the gaps. All the search and selection firms report increased interest on both the demand and supply side.

EXECUTIVE SEARCH FIRMS IN SINGAPORE

International Firms

Amrop (Gattie, Tan Soo Jin)
Boyden
Egon Zehnder
Korn/Ferry
LTA (also operating in Hong Kong)
Russell Reynolds
Strategic Executive Search (a member of Ward Howell International
  Group)

Local Firms

Ed-Lin Associates
Joan Leong Search & Services
Lana Lim & Associates
PHR Group Asia Pacific
R. Anderson & Partners
Richard Glynn Consultants
Young Lai Consultants

Names of Outstanding Consultants

Of the international firms, are Tan Soo Jin and Bob Gattie of Amrop; David Keith of Boyden; Norman Wright of Egon Zehnder; Young Kuan-Sing of Korn/Ferry; Henry Ling of LTA; Annie Wee of Russell Reynolds and Li Hsiao Yuan of Strategic Executive Search. Wright and Ling also operate in the Hong Kong market.

Of the local firms, are Edwin Chan of Ed-Lin; Joan Leong; Lana Lim; Patrick Haro of PHR Group; Ross Siow of R. Anderson & Partners; Richard Glynn; Peter Young Lai.

Sectors of Industry in which Firms Specialise

As in Hong Kong, most firms are generalists, as the Singapore market is too small to justify specialist search services. "The greatest demand is for private bankers, forex traders, corporate financiers, HR professionals for regional jobs, finance directors, tax planners, treasurers, and regional marketing managers in IT and pharmaceuticals", reveals Young Kuan-Sing of Korn/Ferry. LTA's work is 30 per cent financial services and banking. Russell Reynolds do even more searches in financial services: "around 40 per cent", says ex-Citibanker Annie Wee.

As Li Hsiao Yuan of Strategic Executive Search (SES) stresses,

> We are not so heavily into financial services in Singapore since 1984. Only 25–28 per cent of our work is financial. We also search in engineering, manufacturing, high-tech, and marketing. Thirty-five per cent of our assignments are general manager and CEO searches; 30 per cent are for marketing directors, and the rest are in manufacturing and operations, and around 15 per cent are for HR directors, mostly with regional responsibility.

Amrop has a similarly wide spread of assignments. The pattern is similar in Hong Kong, with some firms working predominantly in financial services, others with a wider spread of business.

Average Salary per Assignment

Salary levels are buoyant here. As the Annual Compensation Survey in the April 1994 issue of *World Executive's Digest* showed, salaries of top and senior managers across Asia are highest in Singapore after Tokyo, especially in finance and administration, sales and marketing, and management information systems, where Singapore topped the list.

Korn/Ferry, among the first of the international search firms in Singapore and one of the most active with over ninety searches a year, quotes an average salary of over S$100,000 (US$62,500), a minimum fee of around S$30,000 (US$20,000), with regional jobs commanding premiums, paying S$120,000–180,000 (US$75,000–112,000).

Li Hsiao Yuan of SES reveals that,

> We have assignments with salaries up to S$400,000 (US$250,000). We just placed a thirty-six year old finance director into China

earning this much, with a 30 per cent hardship allowance on top. But our typical searches are at the S$100,000–150,000 level. We carry out around seventy-five assignments a year.

There are slightly fewer searches in Singapore than in Hong Kong, but they are at a similarly high level, in terms of both salaries paid to successful candidates and fees charged to clients. Other cities in Asia (except Tokyo) are far behind.

Advice to Aspiring Executives

"Ten per cent of people who write in get onto short-lists, so it's always worth sending your CV", suggests Young Kuan-Sing of Korn/Ferry. "Executive search is now widely accepted in Singapore, especially among younger executives", adds Annie Wee of Russell Reynolds. "Recently, more and more articles have appeared in the press about search. So making yourself known to a search firm is a wise career move. As one of the more well-known firms, we receive a large number of résumés."

How Important are Academic Qualifications?

Advanced qualifications – such as MBAs – are important, but experience is more so, especially ten to fifteen years' worth. Employers in Singapore are cautious, and above all are looking for a strong track record. Although increasingly, executives in Singapore are studying in the United States and Europe, "it's a myth that you really need an overseas education to get on", insists Tan Soo Jin of Amrop. The local degrees from the National University of Singapore (NUS) and the Singapore Institute of Management (SIM) are highly rated. Yet, "being a graduate is a must", considers Young Kuan-Sing.

Proportion of Women among Placements

This is relatively high (compared with Hong Kong and especially compared with North Asian countries such as Taiwan and Korea), because of high levels of education and an increasing demand for managers. "Women executives are seen by our clients as particularly effective in finance, banking, IT, and HR positions. About 30 per cent of our candidates are women", explains Li Hsiao Yuan of SES.

Proportion of Expatriate and Local Clients

Most search business in Singapore is undertaken on behalf of foreign multinationals, with a very limited domestic market. "Our work is nearly all out of Hong Kong and Singapore because most of our clients are multinationals and they commission out of their Asia head office. Our domestic business is small: only 10 per cent of our business in Hong Kong, and 5 per cent in Singapore", explains Henry Ling of LTA. "Over 65 per cent of our clients are US companies, 25 per cent are European, and the rest – less than 10 per cent – are local", concurs Li Hsiao Yuan of SES. "Now, around 30 per cent of our work is outside of Singapore", he adds.

However, "Singapore is often used as a base for multinational clients setting up in Malaysia, Indonesia and Thailand", explains Annie Wee of Russell Reynolds. As such, the Singapore office of Boyden spawned Boyden offices in Jakarta and Kuala Lumpur, which are sublicensed to Singapore. Just as Hong Kong search firms also operate in Taiwan and China, Singapore-based firms operate in the ASEAN countries. One-third of LTA's business is outside of Hong Kong and Singapore, in China and Taiwan, and Thailand, Malaysia and Indonesia; Ling travels 40 per cent of his time.

Looking towards Other Countries as Sources of Candidates

More and more Asians from outside of Singapore and Western expatriates are knocking at the door; but companies hiring here prefer Singaporeans. "It's hard for expatriates to command a premium any longer. Nine out of ten of our candidates are Singaporeans", insists Young Kuan-Sing, and Tan Soo Jin of Amrop describes a similar picture. "Only about 12 per cent of candidates are Western expatriates", reveals Li Hsiao Yuan of SES. "They are useful for Indonesian assignments, but not necessarily for Singapore. In a typical search we contact at least forty-five people, and they can come from all over the region."

Perceived Competitive Differentiators of Firms

Some Western multinational clients prefer a Western consultant, who nevertheless has much Asian experience. David Keith of Boyden, originally from Britain, has lived all over Asia: "I was sent out by the American ag-chemicals and biotech multinational Monsanto to Thailand, Malaysia, Singapore, Korea and Australia, and came back in 1988 to Singapore." Norman Wright of Egon Zehnder, an American, is one of the few other non-Singaporeans to head-up a search firm here.

Some firms here operate solely in Singapore, undertaking searches for companies based in Singapore, looking for Singaporeans. Others have a wider perspective. LTA, for example, established since 1989 in both Hong Kong and Singapore, see these two locations as one market; they have an informal link with Heidrick & Struggles in the United States, but see themselves as the only independent regional search firm here.

International firms emphasize how they can comb the market regionally through having more offices. "We can also close a job faster, and we offer clients a six-month warranty period", says Young Kuan-Sing of Korn/Ferry. "We are hired by clients who want a global sweep", adds Annie Wee of Russell Reynolds; which was set up in the early 1980s. The Singapore office of Russell Reynolds maintains close contact with the Hong Kong office, which handles its office administration.

Local firms which are nevertheless part of international groupings include Gattie-Tan Soo Jin Consultants (Amrop) and Strategic Executive Search (a member of the Ward Howell International Group). Both their managing directors are ex-international search firms. Tan Soo Jin previously worked for Korn/Ferry and Egon Zehnder, and Li Hsiao Yuan of SES joined his firm from Korn/Ferry, in 1986. They emphasize their contrasts with the big branded networks: "we are independent operators, and more selective about which clients we want to work for, and we are not driven by head office revenue requirements, and we are not told what to do by distant senior partners", insists Tan Soo Jin.

CLIENT COMMENTS

A large search user in the banking sector comments,

> The choice between good search firms in Singapore is not large, but there are some quality firms around. It depends on the particular search. If you want to pull in a global high-flyer, then probably Russell Reynolds or Korn/Ferry would be a good choice. Egon Zehnder don't seem to be particularly strong in this area. For a local Singaporean or for candidates from around the region, I've found that Li Hsiao Yuan and Tan Soo Jin, in particular, do a good job.

"We have had a problem with finding a search firm which still has places in which to hunt," admits a multinational securities firm, "and this is especially true in a small market like Singapore. We were attracted to LTA, with their relatively short client list." ("We have less than seventy clients in Hong Kong and Singapore, nearly all of them Fortune 200 companies", says Henry Ling). "Bearing in mind that they are not supposed to take people out of client companies, this means they have less of an off-limits problem", explains the client.

ADVERTISED RECRUITMENT/ SELECTION IN THIS MARKET

The most active firms in the selection market in Singapore, judging by published job ads over the last six months, would appear to be KPMG Peat Marwick, Price Waterhouse, Coopers & Lybrand and the PA Consulting Group, followed by Ernst & Young and local firms EO and Tiro. There are many other smaller players, often international firms who, in many cases, are more active elsewhere (such as Drake in Hong Kong). Selection is more seasonal than executive search. December and January are often slow, but business tends to pick up during February to March, especially after year-end bonuses have been received, when vacancies can occur. July to August can be quiet again.

Although predominantly advertising for candidates, most selection firms welcome résumés by mail.

Bruce Hunt of KPMG Peat Marwick explains that,

> Often we carry out a database search before placing an ad, in case the position can be filled this way. This can save the client the cost of an ad. Or we may do both. It's unlikely that we would jump straight into an ad without a database search first.

Cheah Chew Ping of Price Waterhouse also makes use of her firm's database: "about 30 per cent of my work is by database search. We keep the names of candidates from previous assignments, and from unsolicited CVs. We find that some clients are in a hurry, and can't wait for an ad. The database helps them to make a quick placement." But buyers of this sort of recruitment service should be wary of selection firms with massive databases. They may not have been 'cleaned' recently, and much of the information may be outdated.

The CPA firms have generalist businesses, but usually 45–50 per cent of their work is in finance. "More than 60 per cent of our clients are from the auditing side", explains Cheah Chew Ping. These firms often charge fees according to the time taken, at a fixed hourly charge-out rate, or a proportion of the salary of the successful candidate.

In the selection business in Singapore, 1989–90 was a boom time, 1991 was quiet, 1992 and 1993 were better, and 1994 saw business picking up, "the product of the setting up of more regional offices in Singapore by multinationals, and subsequent infilling", suggests Cheah Chew Ping. She has also seen increased numbers in response to ads: it used to be between 40–60, and now it's between 100–150. The increase is not made up of local Singaporeans, but of people from around the region, especially people of Chinese origin from Australia and New Zealand, together with Malaysians and Indians. There has been a big rise in expatriate applications from Europe, with people coming "on spec" looking for jobs.

"However, we look for locals first, and if can't find them in Singapore, then we look in Malaysia and the Philippines, but this takes longer", explains Eddie Sung of PA.

Overall, the selection business in Singapore is becoming more sophisticated. "We have noticed increased demand for psychological testing and other services. Clients are more demanding, they know how to shop around, and they want faster and more reliable service. If you can offer what they want, it's very profitable", considers Sung.

SELECTION

International Firms

Arthur Andersen Associates
Berkeley Executive Resources (affiliated with MSL in the United Kingdom)
Blue Arrow Consultants
Business Trends
Coopers & Lybrand
Deloitte & Touche Management Consultants
Drake Executive
Ernst & Young
KPMG Peat Marwick
PA Consulting Group
Price Waterhouse Management Consultants

Local Firms

CEO Search & Services
Chevron Consulting Services
D. P. Search
Dolly Poh & Associates
E. R. Executive Recruiters
EO Consulting Services
ExeQuest Management Consultants
Gary Ng Management Consultants
Job-Match International
Johnson & Mah
Management Search
Pacific Management Resources
SS&A Management Consultants
Tiro Consulting Services

CHAPTER 8

MALAYSIA

Relaxation of Work Permit Restrictions

Malaysia's supply of managers is now far outstripped by demand, forcing up salaries and freeing up the job market; meanwhile, the emergence of recruitment services lags behind.

Malaysia is moving rapidly towards achieving its 'industrialisation by 2020' goal, but the shortage of managers is potentially inhibiting this. Salaries are rising, but training and staff development are needed to fit executives for more senior jobs. Work permit regulations are being relaxed, so the job market is likely to become more pan-Asian in the future.

Executive search and selection services are still fairly thin on the ground, probably a result of the comparatively low level of salaries at the moment. So if you are looking for a career move within Malaysia or looking for a job in Malaysia from outside, there are not so many search and selection firms to approach. Again, remember that they're client-driven and their clients are employers, not individuals looking for a job, but they are all keen to build up their databases. Prepare to take a salary cut if you are coming from Hong Kong, Singapore or Taiwan; expect more money if you are coming from the Philippines, Indonesia or Thailand. And remember that the cost of living in Malaysia is one of the lowest in Asia, and opportunities are wide open. Bonuses can be bigger than salaries, so pay particular attention to this when negotiating a remuneration package. There is no clear distinction between search and selection in this market, and most firms are in both.

In particular demand in Malaysia are general and regional managers, human resource managers, computer marketing managers, engineers, technical specialists, accountants, trainers and consultants and EDP managers. There are few job areas which do not need more people, but lawyers and financial services executives are in less demand.

Employers and job seekers should be aware of the restrictions on entering Malaysia, however, and the fact that the Government seeks to encourage ethnic Malays above others in job opportunities. Yet in practice it is a very mixed society and business community, with a preponderance of Chinese and Indians, as well as Malays.

EXECUTIVE SEARCH FIRMS IN MALAYSIA

International Firms

Korn/Ferry
Coopers & Lybrand
PA Consulting Group
KPMG Peat Marwick Management Consultants
Price Waterhouse Management Consulting Services
TAO [Teams and Organization] (also in Hong Kong, Taiwan and Korea)

Local Firms

PLC Partners Consulting
Organization Renewal Inc.
David W. Buker (ASEAN)

Names of Outstanding Consultants

Of the international firms, are Anne Venus of Korn/Ferry; Munira Salinger of Coopers & Lybrand; Henry Lee of PA; Jagan Sabapathy of Peat Marwick; M. Noor Ghani and Robert Lim of Price Waterhouse; Augustin Coppey and Roselyn Tee of TAO.

Of the local firms, Lin Wai Ling of PLC Partners Consulting; Irene Tan of Organization Renewal Inc.; and David Buker of David W. Buker (ASEAN).

Sectors of Industry in which Firms Specialise

Korn/Ferry have a generalist practice in Kuala Lumpur. "The firm here is too small for the consultants to specialise", reflects managing partner Anne Venus; "Malaysia is still a small market from the search point of view." Consumer products, retail, Fast Moving Consumer Goods, electrical, electronics, manufacturing, construction, chemicals, and pharmaceuticals are important areas for Korn/Ferry, together with functional areas such as general managers, and human resources and public relations professionals. "We have a good general business", Venus continues, "there's hardly anything we don't cover, although financial services is the smallest part of our business." Venus finds that the most mobile executives are in IT. There is more familiarity with being headhunted in IT, and in consumer marketing, but in other areas search is more unusual. TAO, according to Augustin Coppey, also has a generalist practice.

Price Waterhouse, by contrast, has a lot of work in financial services. But there are limits here. "You mustn't steal people from the Central Bank", explains M. Noor Ghani, Executive Director of Management Consulting Services. "All banks coming in have to have approval from Central Bank", he continues. "This blocks out a big recruitment area for us, with no mainstream banking searches. But we can headhunt in insurance and leasing and other financial areas, and also in manufacturing, engineering, technical specialists and commercial trading", adds Robert Lim, a manager in Noor Ghani's department. In manufacturing, Price Waterhouse recruits from general managers and managing directors downwards, placing managers in production, personnel, and quality control, especially for new investors entering the Malaysian market, such as Taiwanese and Japanese companies.

Average Salary per Assignment

Salary levels in the city of Kuala Lumpur, analysed in the Annual Compensation Survey found in the April 1994 issue of *World Executive's Digest*, are about midway between the highest and lowest in Asia; they've doubled over the last five years. Junior managers in Kuala Lumpur earn around US$14,500, compared with US$26,000 in Taipei, but only US$7,000 in Manila. Middle managers have crept up to US$32,000 (Taipei US$42,500 and Manila US$14,000) whilst senior managers in Kuala Lumpur receive approximately US$70,000 (Singapore US$85,000 and Manila US$28,000). However, the cost of living in Kuala Lumpur is significantly lower than in Hong Kong, Taipei, Singapore or Seoul. As the shortage of managers intensifies, salaries are expected to continue to rise.

The search firms questioned agree that salaries are increasing dramatically, reflecting the shortage of good people in all areas. Korn/ Ferry starts at around M$90,000 at general manager level, up to M$250,000 for more senior executives. "Malaysia is one of the cheapest places in Asia to employ executives," Venus considers, "but there are lots of opportunities for big bonuses, as companies try to minimise their fixed overheads." TAO has a similar experience here. Price Waterhouse quotes an average salary level in search of M$120,000, and PA around M$100,000 and above.

Advice to Aspiring Executives

Korn/Ferry has an extensive database of write-ins. "We don't discourage these but we don't encourage them either", explains Venus. "It's hard to make people here understand that we aren't here to find them jobs." Her firm's candidates are 95 per cent local, but may be of Indian or Chinese ethnicity as well as Malay. She would always consider really good candidates from outside Malaysia who don't mind being relocated. She warns against moving too often.

> Most people here won't move if they find a good employer. Loyalty is more important here than in Hong Kong, for example. People don't leave easily even if they're offered big sums. Someone moving every one to two years would be seen as job-hopping. If you're 35 to 40, three jobs would be enough. You may have more jobs if you're in IT, a technical position, or a project-oriented job. But this is a very traditional place. For this reason, it's surprising that we do so much business, although this is a result of the expansion of the economy.

In building up a database, the firm finds it doesn't change so quickly as in other markets. "You can easily identify people here, but there is a need for more quality managers, and we've seen a big expansion of demand." TAO, according to research manager Roselyn Tee, has also developed a large database, partly to offset the lack of published research sources.

Price Waterhouse – and other firms – find that networking in the market-place is used for senior-level jobs, with search mostly confined to middle management. So very senior managers won't necessarily move this way. Their candidates are also mostly local, given the issue of work permit problems, but this situation is changing, and permit rules are less stringent. They hire only three to four expatriates per year. Noor Ghani echoes Venus in saying "you must stay in your job for four to five years or you'll get a black mark."

PA notes that there are plentiful employment oportunities here across the board, including regional jobs.

There is a dearth of good people here, but it's largely a local market, although this may change, especially if salaries continue to rise. There are big gaps in the junior management level, especially as there is not so much mobility.

How Important are Academic Qualifications?

Korn/Ferry sees an MBA degree as an advantage for marketing managers, financial controllers and in consulting.

Venus reveals that,

Overall, it's seen as an indication of serious intent. Most MBAs here are gained through Distance Learning courses, taking two to three years. There's no preference for MBAs from the United States or United Kingdom, necessarily. But most of our clients express a preference for practical experience, and relevant practical qualifications. Unfortunately, one of the problems in Malaysia is that 70 per cent of university students here are studying social sciences and arts, when they should be in engineering, and the practical subjects the country needs.

Price Waterhouse haven't asked candidates for MBAs much in the past, but now they're starting to, and contrary to Korn/Ferry, they prefer an overseas education.

Lim explains,

Fifty thousand Malaysians are studying all over the world. More people are educated overseas than locally, and they're in a better position, with higher standards of English. The local universities mostly teach in Malay, so it's preferable to go overseas to get a more international outlook.

PA also finds MBAs to be incidental, and that practical experience is more relevant.

Henry Lee suggests,

Employers like an MBA but it's not essential. It doesn't automatically get you places, but it improves polish and maturity. An overseas education is socially more acceptable, but this is mostly not an issue to employers.

Proportion of Expatriate and Local Clients

Korn/Ferry's clients are 70 per cent multinational; they find that relatively few local companies use consulting services. However, they've seen substantial growth in search every year, with more local companies using search, although these businesses tend to use local recruitment services where billing arrangements may be more attractive. Local search firms seem to be able to penetrate the local market more effectively than the international firms, especially as the latter tend to charge higher fees. Clients across Malaysia are becoming more familiar with search, and can appreciate the differences between search and selection/advertising. Venus also feels that most senior appointments in Malaysia – for multinationals or local companies – are completed through invitation rather than search. Multinationals bring in expatriates and, for local companies, in the small business community, people know each other. Price Waterhouse has a balance of multinational and local clients, of around fifty/fifty. PA has a majority of multinational clients: "they've heard of us."

Proportion of Women among Placements

Both Korn/Ferry and TAO have placed some women candidates. They tend to be mostly Chinese, and in human resources, general consulting, or accounting. These areas would attract one in five women candidates. But they are not in production engineering, or very senior roles. Price Waterhouse come across few women candidates, but some in human resources, advertising, as financial controllers, and in communications. PA have placed more women candidates, and many of their own consultants are women.

Perceived Competitive Differentiators of Firms

Many users of search appreciate a firm which has been in the market a long time and which has built up a good deal of market knowledge. Korn/Ferry in Malaysia has been around for fourteen years, opening a formal office eight years ago. At this point, Malaysia was in recession, and there were no jobs; but Venus pioneered the marketing of search, so that when the economy picked up, Korn/Ferry was able to attract a lot of business, and has now developed a strong market-leading position. With no other large branded search firms in Kuala Lumpur, they dominate the top of the market. Korn/Ferry has four senior consultants with support staff, but the consultants do much of their own research. They maintain that "there's a shortage of good people here, but we can always produce good candidates." They have some repeat business, although companies are often small, and there are not many senior positions which require search. New business comes mostly through referrals.

TAO is a newer firm in this market, having been originally started by a Frenchman in Korea. They see themselves as young and dynamic, with original ideas, and with the strength of a region-wide network behind them. Price Waterhouse is a highly-respected name among CPA firms. They claim to concentrate on search, with four consultants, but offer a range of other human resource services, such as remuneration surveys (as do PA). They recruit for a wide variety of positions, from managing directors and general managers down to sales representatives, a much broader spectrum than Korn/Ferry. Their auditing business is a restriction in search, as they cannot approach people working in client companies, but it's alright if they write in. (The same is true for Coopers & Lybrand and for Peat Marwick). PA has been in Kuala Lumpur since 1968, and claim to have started their search business soon after. With five or six consultants doing search and selection, this part of their business took off around five years ago. They gained more and more clients as the market for good executives became tighter in Malaysia's economic boom. PA claim 60–70 per cent repeat business. They charge around 30 per cent of the salary payable to the successful candidate, whereas Korn/Ferry charges 35 per cent. The biggest problem in search here, according to PA, is that a client delays making a decision and loses the candidate, because he gets a counter-offer from his existing company.

CLIENT COMMENTS

We've come to Korn/Ferry after advertisements have failed to produce the candidates we want. Apparently, this is true of 20 per cent of their searches. We find that sometimes, advertising is not that effective at the senior level; some people are reluctant to respond to ads because of their need for confidentiality. However, we find Korn/Ferry to be trustworthy and discreet, whereas leaks have been known to occur from other firms. Candidates worry about appearing to be disloyal, and we wouldn't want people who didn't. It's a small market here, and there's a need for discretion, even more for candidates than for us.

As a multinational company, we have used search in a number of markets, but we didn't expect to be able to find search services here. There aren't many firms, but they include some good quality operations. The CPA firms offer a professional service, and they don't try to kid us that it will be easy to find what we want. This is an exciting market for us, but our growth here could be hampered by the shortage of good people.

ADVERTISED RECRUITMENT/ SELECTION IN THIS MARKET

International Firms

Business Trends (now BTI) Consultants (also in Singapore and Indonesia)
Coopers & Lybrand Management Consultancy Services
Ernst & Young
Norconsult K.L.
PA Consulting Group
KPMG Peat Marwick Management Consultants
Price Waterhouse Management Consulting Services
TAO [Teams and Organization] (also in Hong Kong, Taiwan and Korea)

Local Firms

PLC Partners Consulting
Organization Renewal Inc.
David W. Buker (ASEAN)

Most of the executive recruitment firms in Kuala Lumpur carry out both search and selection; Korn/Ferry is the only firm concerned exclusively with search. Coopers & Lybrand, Peat Marwick and Price Waterhouse do some search, but are more concerned with advertising. The last of this list's business is sixty/forty selection to search. Price Waterhouse see themselves as the largest in advertising, followed by PA (but PA do more search than the others, and TAO are also mostly involved in search). They see Business Trends (BTI) as at a lower level. "We advertise even for M$300,000 jobs, as we think the way we write the advertisement attracts even the most top guys", Price Waterhouse claim. They use selection to augment their search services. "We find an initial core group and then we help them to staff up, through ads, for more junior people. Most of our selection work is in finance and accounting, then production. We use selection for jobs from M$120,000 downwards to a minimum of M$40,000." Coopers & Lybrand and KPMG Peat Marwick are also strong in selection. The median for job salary for ads is M$70,000.

Business Trends, now known as BTI, was set up first in Singapore, then opened in Malaysia in 1985, offering a wide range of recruiting services. They also have an office in Jakarta (their work in Kuala Lumpur includes one to three assignments on a regional basis per month). Director Kal Randhawa claims that 90 per cent of their clients are multinationals, with some work for local companies, and US non-profit organisations: "BTI can handle project recruitment of teams, from the

93

lowest to highest level", including non-retainer database search and cold-calling. "We recommend job ads as being good for the image of a company too," considers Randhawa, "but we recognise that others want to be discreet. Lots of our clients are expatriates, but Asians are increasingly learning about recruitment services." Their range of recruiting expertise is such that they carry out an average of seven to eight jobs per client per year (at a higher level, it would be unlikely that one company would have so many vacancies). BTI have a large database, for both file search and selection, always identifying people on the database first, before carrying out sourcing in the market.

Randhawa points to the need for training and upgrading of skills in Malaysia, and the lack of real quality people.

> If we put out a job ad for a sales and marketing manager, we would get as many as seventy to eighty replies, but only ten would be really good. The problem here is that many people are promoted without the necessary skills and experience, because there's such a shortage, then they think they can do jobs which really require more than they can offer.

Randhawa agrees that if you have moved more than say five times by the time you're 35, you will have a big problem moving again, and that the most successful people tend to stay in the same industry.

BTI sees engineering as suffering the most severe shortages, especially in areas of construction, roads, and marine. More women are coming into office management, but lots of clients would rather deal with male managers. Salary levels handled by BTI are from M$15,000 to M$18,000 per month, and can go up to M$20,000, even to CEO salary levels of M$250,000. Ad work can be as low as M$3,000 per month. BTI finds some resistance to employing Malaysians who have gone overseas, although Malaysian people are increasingly mobile, going to Singapore, Indonesia and Hong Kong. BTI charges fees from 18–25 per cent of the salary of the successful candidate (compared with 30–35 per cent in search); other firms in the selection market charge only 15–18 per cent. They offer a special rate for regular clients, and a service fee upfront from a new client, but this is not a retainer.

Salaries of advertised jobs have risen 55 per cent in Malaysia since 1988, when the country came out of recession. It is expected that there will continue to be a big demand in oil and gas, and construction. There could be an increase in contract managers, but many people don't want contract jobs so much. There is a good climate for jobs right now in Malaysia, but people need to upgrade their skills, and become specialists in the various areas of demand.

CHAPTER 9

THAILAND

Only Thais Need Apply

Career opportunities – and salaries – are booming in Thailand, but continuing restrictions mean that work permits for foreigners, Western and Asian, are in short supply.

With more and more multinationals arriving, joint-ventures being formed and local conglomerates on the rise, Thailand is booming and, with GDP growth still at 7 per cent, the demand for management talent far exceeds supply. But of all Asian commercial centres, Bangkok is the most restricted in terms of allowing the free entry of executives from outside. However, there are important exceptions and, for those who can make it, time spent in Thailand is stimulating and rewarding, and understanding Thailand should be an important part of any Asian manager's pan-regional experience.

Meanwhile, Thai executives are rising to the challenge of the boom in local commercial activity, and are rapidly replacing expatriates, even in many prominent multinationals.

Bangkok is increasingly the only place to work in Thailand, despite efforts to develop other towns. It is expected that in the next decade, 40 per cent of all industry will be in Bangkok. The chronic traffic situation has made people more conscious of where they are working and living, since it is very frustrating to get to and from work. Four hours of commuting per day is almost minimal, and higher-income families live nearer to their workplace and in the suburbs, to beat the traffic. It's not unknown for on-the-move executives to have two carphones (for incoming and outgoing calls), a car fax machine, laptop computer and portable television, to say nothing of thermos flasks and sandwiches. If the car can't get to the office, then the office must come to the car!

EXECUTIVE SEARCH AND RECRUITMENT FIRMS IN THAILAND

Korn/Ferry International, Executive Recruitment (Thailand) Ltd.
Boyden Associates (Thailand) Ltd.
Price Waterhouse, Management Consultants Ltd.
Coopers & Lybrand Executive Selection Services
Merc (an associate of PA)
SGV/Arthur Andersen Executive Recruitment Services Ltd.
KPMG Peat Marwick
Ernst & Young
BDO Executive Recruitment Services
Prompt Professional Resources & Services Co. Ltd.

Sectors of Industry in which Firms Specialise

The areas in which executives are in demand in Thailand are high-technology, sales and marketing, computing, telecommunications, finance, securities, banking, manufacturing, and consumer products. Pharmaceuticals and health care are important areas, as is construction, although the construction industry is now ahead of itself, and there is an oversupply now of buildings and office space. (This has brought down rents, favouring companies coming into Bangkok; central rents used to be around 800 baht per square metre, but is now around 500 baht per square metre.)

In 1991 and 1992, the manufacturing sector began tailing off, but there was increased demand in accounting, finance, human resources, computing, public relations – in the service and support aspects of companies – as many businesses are consolidating internally. These are often prime targets for non-Thai executives wanting to work in Bangkok (except accounting which is reserved for Thais). In 1994–5 Thailand's economy continues to grow, identified as the fastest-growing in Asia, according to *Asia Inc.* magazine.

Average Salary per Assignment

Such is the dynamics of the demand and supply situation, that salaries are rapidly increasing, and there are some accusations that some people are overpaid because of the shortage. But certainly Thailand is coming up to the level of other Asian countries such as Hong Kong, Singapore and Taiwan. In April 1994, Bangkok salaries exceeded Jakarta and Manila, according to Corporate Resources Group's findings, reaching the levels of Seoul and Kuala Lumpur. Commentators suggest a rise of at least 10–15 per cent over the last year. Amrop International, in their survey of round-the-region budgeted salary increases, put Thailand rises at 7–10 per cent for 1994.

As Arunee Vidhayasirinun of Korn/Ferry reveals,

> There have been many incidences when I've placed a person, especially in finance, at double their salary. In the early 1980s, salaries were quite low in Bangkok, only one-half to one-third of what they would get in Hong Kong or Singapore. But managers in Thailand are earning around 75 per cent or 80 per cent of the top-paying places like Hong Kong.

This big jump in salaries is a function of the scarcity of employees and the increasing perception that a Thai national can do a job just as well as an expatriate. Thai salaries are increasing as a result.

Top executives in the private sector can earn up to 400,000 baht per month. Annual reviews carried out by companies on their employees are now held twice a year, rather than once, and a 10–20 per cent pay rise is often awarded after only six months. A rise of less than 10 per cent per year is seen as too low. Many multinationals are shocked at this (paying only 2–3 per cent rises per year in the US head office). But locals still earn only half the amount of Western expatriates in many cases.

Performance bonuses are spread out over the year in an effort to stop people from leaving *en masse* when they're received. So Christmas and Chinese New Year bonuses are given out, and a midyear performance bonus too. Cars and overseas business trips provide a big incentive to stay, and many companies are sending people on overseas Master's programmes. The Thai Farmers' Bank sends senior managers to Wharton, Siam Cement send theirs to Harvard for senior executive management programmes.

Advice to Aspiring Executives

Chainarong Indharameesup of Boyden's advice to people from outside, looking for employment opportunities in Thailand, is that there are really three possibilities: the multinational companies; the joint-ventures between multinational and locals; and the local operations. Multinationals should be a prime target for outsiders, and many multinationals advertise positions possibly open to non-Thais. However, there are less than 2,000 multinationals in Thailand, and they only have small quotas of non-Thais. Joint-ventures employ non-Thais according to the nationality of the foreign partner, but they usually bring their own staff with them. Local companies use non-Thais in specific areas where they lack expertise, which could include general manager roles. But many local, family-owned companies are training the next generation and there may be fewer openings here.

Mobility and Retention of Executives

Younger Thai executives are now looking to move up quickly. Older ones tend to be more loyal to their employers (and most of the search firms' candidates fall into this age group). Many are finding that they can get a 30–50 per cent increase when they move jobs after about two or three years in a company. A stay of two or three years is the norm.

A client of Price Waterhouse comments,

> If they stay a short time, they don't learn so much about the company or the job, which is one of the problems of job-hopping. And companies are getting worried about people moving too much. It does happen that people leave after only a year for double salary.

In areas like marketing, a company which gets three or four years out of a person is doing quite well. In Japanese companies, there is much more of a sense of loyalty, and longer periods of employment with the same employer. In the top groups in Thailand, such as Siam Cement, people stay longer, because the training provided is very good, as in the case of another leading conglomerate, Charoen Pokphand. Leading multinationals such as Esso and Shell tend to retain people too, especially because they offer attractive incentives matching years of service.

Thai executives often jump between industries and become good generalists: they have a moral issue about leaving a company and working for competitors, and because of this they are more likely to move between different industries so they are not accused of defecting to competitors.

With this increased mobility, the pool is shrinking, and all headhunters are fighting over the same people. When the best candidates are on the market, they have five or six job offers. After one year, they can move again, and again get several job offers.

How Important are Academic Qualifications?

An ideal candidate for an executive posting in Bangkok would be a Thai with an overseas education and multinational experience. The qualifications needed in foreign candidates must be in areas in which Thais don't have the expertise, as well as all of the above. A good local education is acceptable, as long as it's with a good university, such as Chulalongkorn or Thammasat. The English language is in reasonably high demand, but Thailand is not officially an English-speaking country. The spread of English is not as wide as in Malaysia and Singapore for example.

Thai-speakers are in demand because the Thai language is used in most offices. English is used in multinationals, but Thais speak together in Thai. "It's not just knowing the language. It's about being a Thai; going to school and college together, having networks among your families", explains Arunee. "It's a very aristocrat-dominated society, and it would be very hard for a foreigner to network as well and as effectively as high-ranking Thais can network."

The search firms see it as a considerable advantage to have an MBA. The standard of students is high in Thailand in the better schools, because competition for entry is so intense. Most recruiters in Thailand argue that the top universities in Thailand are as good as the top twenty in the United States. There is a huge amount of interest in higher education in Thailand. "Many candidates have three or four degrees", describes Price Waterhouse. "They may have something like an accounting degree, plus a diploma in auditing, and they've studied in the evening and have completed an MBA." Jarunee Sathirangkul of Price Waterhouse adds that there are more women than ever in the graduate school programmes, and they are rapidly improving their chances of getting top appointments.

Employers are looking particularly for experience of working in multinationals, and being able to understand cultural differences and sensitivities; people who have worked in these companies are seen as having a broader outlook, and a more international approach. Often a Japanese client will look for a candidate who has worked in a Japanese company before, and newly-established American companies prefer people with US education and work experience. "They like this sort of thing so much that they'd even put it in an advertisement", reveals Price Waterhouse.

Proportion of Expatriate and Local Clients

Ninety per cent of Korn/Ferry's clients are foreign companies looking to set up or expand their businesses in Thailand. There is no enormous demand yet from Thai companies. The profile of the Thai search market is similar to that in Japan, where local executives are in demand as candidates, but nearly all the clients are foreign multinationals. "Even some of the American companies operating companies in Thailand are not used to search, but they are having to use it because of the enormous shortage of managers here", explains Chainarong of Boyden. He finds that Thai companies are beginning to use search more and more, and estimates that his business is 70 per cent foreign and 30 per cent Thai, in contrast to Korn/Ferry's more foreign-dominated business.

The joint-ventures in Thailand, in number, are ten times bigger than the multinational groups, but individually they're smaller. The most popular joint-ventures are with Japanese companies, as well as Korean, Taiwanese and Indonesian. They are geared towards hiring managers of the nationality of the joint-venture; for example, Japanese joint-ventures want Japanese people.

Looking towards Other Countries as Sources of Candidates

Of a total population of probably around 58 million in Thailand, there may be 100,000–200,000 foreigners in Thailand, much less than in Hong Kong or Singapore. The expatriate population is dominated by around 20,000 Japanese. Third- or fourth-generation Thai Chinese make up an estimated 50 per cent of the population of Bangkok.

It must be emphasized from the outset (according to Bruce Clarke of Price Waterhouse) that it's not easy to work as a non-Thai in Bangkok. It's much more difficult in Thailand than it would be in Malaysia or Indonesia to get in as a non-local. Only foreigners in specific areas of shortage – such as engineering, architecture, computer science and financial services – can be admitted. Non-Thais have to get work permits – which can be difficult – and they have to get their company to sponsor them, since it is not possible to obtain a work permit as individuals.

However, some companies recruit Singaporeans or Hong Kong Chinese, especially in finance, Filipinos in marketing and finance, and Indians in technical roles, or any of them can be in general manager or country manager roles. There are not enough Thais with financial experience, and also not enough Thais to run large department stores and shopping plazas, and on the Fast Moving Consumer Goods side. "It's not that we as Thais don't have the knowledge," points out Arunee, "but we just don't have enough trained and experienced people, due to the fast growth in Thailand over the last five years." In the three years in which Korn/Ferry has been operating in Bangkok, all successful placements have been Thais, except for one American, as a regional manager for an American company working in Thailand.

There are many expatriates in Thailand's big pharmaceutical industry, especially in marketing and distribution. There are many Hong Kong and Singaporean Chinese working in manufacturing, in toys, textiles, plastics, petrochemicals and computers. Some foreigners settle down in Thailand, get residency and then Thai nationality in due course. If they have the money and the contacts, this takes five to seven years.

So bringing in expatriates – Western or Asian – is quite a nightmare for companies legally, and there is the financial issue of foreigners expecting expatriate packages, including housing allowances, etc. It's cheaper, as in most cases in Asia, to get a local person. Arunee has found that sometimes expatriates come in saying they don't mind having a local package and agree to be a local hire, but as soon as they actually come in, they start asking for more, such as housing, special salary benefits, and other expatriate perks. Also, non-Thais can only succeed if their jobs can be done without all the necessary language skills and networking connections.

It is easier to bring foreigners in on short-term assignments, and this specifically applies to the Hong Kong and Singaporean Chinese. These include people who have been trained in the financial services sector, in swaps, foreign exchange and different kinds of financial instruments, and have new ideas on project financing, areas in which Thais have little knowledge. Short-term assignments of foreigners are quite acceptable by the authorities, especially for overseas-funded government projects.

Foreign multinationals used to bring their own people into Thailand, but are now developing local staff; "everyone wants local staff now", insists Chainarong. Most expatriates have been transferred from head-offices, not recruited locally, and even foreign companies don't have many foreign executives now. And they're promoting Thais to senior positions. Thirachai, the Managing Director of DuPont in Bangkok, is also on the DuPont world board. Kamthorn, Chairman of Lintas Asia-Pacific, is also on the Lintas world board. Some are replacing senior Western expatriates with Asian expatriates: Dow Corning has a Taiwanese country manager in Bangkok. He's cheaper than an American, more aggressive than a Thai, and has better English.

Meanwhile, Thais themselves are working in other countries, as some factories are moving out, to the Philippines, Indonesia, Vietnam and the People's Republic of China, as Thai labour costs are rising. With this, there is also a growing tendency to export Thai managers to Indo-China, Indonesia and the People's Republic of China, and to run – for example – Australian companies in Papua New Guinea (as in a recent assignment undertaken by Price Waterhouse). Thais can cope with climate problems and get on with the labour force quite easily. Thais are also good for working in the Middle East (there are many Thai Moslems, perhaps 5 per cent of the population).

Perceived Competitive Differentiators of Firms

The demand for executives in Bangkok has led to the emergence of several new start-up search firms. As a result, many established firms, and users of search, feel that there has been a decline in the quality of recruitment in the market.

Korn/Ferry started in Bangkok three years ago. Previously, their work here was carried out from Singapore and Hong Kong, but "Korn/Ferry can serve its clients better if they know we're on the spot", argues managing director Arunee Vidhayasirinun, headhunted by Korn/Ferry in Singapore from American Express to head-up the Bangkok office.

Boyden has been in Bangkok for nearly ten years, initially attracted by the mid-1980s boom in manufacturing, when many foreign joint-ventures started up, and factories were established in Thailand by Japanese and American companies, among others. Chainarong Indharameesup set up the office as an offshoot of Boyden's Singapore branch, and was one of the first executives to do international style executive search in Thailand. Like Korn/Ferry, Boyden works at the higher levels, searching for country managers and functional directors. "When I set up this business, no one had heard of executive search", he recalls. "And there is still some confusion in the Bangkok market-place between recruitment and search, and between well-established international firms and new start-ups" he continues. Of the international firms in Bangkok, only Korn/Ferry and Boyden are on the ground. Russell Reynolds search here out of Hong Kong, and to a lesser extent Spencer Stuart and Egon Zehnder.

Fees Charged by Search Firms

Boyden and Korn/Ferry insist on fees of one-third of the successful candidate's first year remuneration, on a retainer basis, with a minimum fee of US$10,000–12,000.

Price Waterhouse seldom handle jobs under 40,000 baht per month, and the range is up to 250,000 baht per month. This would be a salary for a senior executive in financial services, which puts them right up into the Western league. An MD of a merchant bank in Bangkok is earning roughly 60 per cent of UK salary on that level, with bonuses of at least 50 per cent of the salary.

For advertised recruitment vacancies, Price Waterhouse charge 18 per cent, for search assignments one-third, plus expenses and the price of the advertisements. "Many local Thai companies think they can recruit more cheaply on their own," Price Waterhouse comments, "and also they're too used to getting free referrals. But the shortage of managers means that this situation is changing."

CLIENT COMMENTS

A large financial services user feels that,

> although now threatened by many new small entrants, there's been an increase in quality as time has gone on in the search business here, and Korn/Ferry in particular has become a leader in the professional end of the search market in Bangkok.

A multinational trading company comments that,

> one of the reasons for the growth of search firms here has been the rise of local executives. Many US and other foreign companies don't necessarily know how to get these local executives, and really only the search firms can give us what they want, at the higher level. Boyden and Korn/Ferry are the only two companies in Bangkok involved in international executive search.

A financial services user of search explains that,

> SGV is the largest auditing firm in Bangkok, and was the first CPA firm to enter recruitment, followed by Coopers & Lybrand, then Price Waterhouse. Deloitte has a joint-venture here, but it doesn't seem to be so active.

SELECTION FIRMS IN THAILAND

The major CPA firms are all active in advertised selection here. The PA Consulting Group is represented in Bangkok through Merc, their associate; they were the first recruitment firm to set up here. Price Waterhouse, Coopers & Lybrand and Ernst & Young soon followed. SGV – the local auditing market leader – in association with Arthur Andersen was particularly strong at the beginning, but is now less so. KPMG Peat Marwick entered the recruitment market recently.

Chainarong suggests that,

> The CPA firms have a captive market in advertised recruitment. Through their work on the auditing side of the business, they know

what's happening in their clients' companies, and when they need executives.

There are other less active selection firms, often run by ex-consultants of the search firms and the CPA firms. These are local companies, but they have some international affiliations. They include EMI and Personnel Recruitment Consultants (PRC), three or four boutique firms advertising for executives in the retail business and real estate, and 'one-line' agencies, i.e. they describe the job in one line in the newspaper. These are all working on contingency. The CPA firms are expanding their operations. Price Waterhouse is typical. Their volume of work in recruitment has increased considerably from when it first entered this business. However, these firms complain,

> it's harder and harder to find appropriately qualified, trained people to handle positions we have available. Many of the candidates going into jobs are really too young to do the job particularly well, because there's such a short supply of qualified people.

Over 60 per cent of Price Waterhouse's work is advertised recruitment, so there is a only a relatively small amount of headhunting work, as in the case of the other CPA firms.

CHAPTER 10
PHILIPPINES

Go Overseas to Seek Your Fortune

Multinationals make attractive employers in the Philippines; otherwise, opportunities outside, throughout the region, are beckoning Filipino managers to leave home and they make successful expatriates.

The lack of progress in the Philippine economy and the relatively low level of salaries is deterring managers elsewhere in the region from looking for opportunities here. Meanwhile, some of the most able Filipino managers are exporting themselves, attracted by the perks of expatriate status and, with good language skills and ease of mobility, they are increasingly in demand. However, working for branches of multinationals in the Philippines is still very attractive, because of the promise of higher than usual salaries and opportunities for speedy promotion and overseas travel.

"Many Filipinos are looking for jobs outside. They're seen as more rewarding, with perks such as free education for their children", explains Nanette Dollente, of Corporate Search Professionals in Manila.

105

They look to leave for two to three years, then return after having made substantial savings. There are not many opportunities in Philippines with the economy not doing so well. Investors are apprehensive, but there is a more positive outlook with initiatives such as Philippines 2000. But those executives currently with big multinationals are staying on, as they can earn good salaries.

With commercial activity and salaries at a comparatively low level, there is no large demand for executive search in the Philippines. Jesus ('Giji') Zulueta of W. D. Scott points out that 95 per cent of businesses in the Philippines are owner-managed, and they're not used to using search firms. "There is a need to educate clients," he says, "since very few companies in the Philippines use search, except multinationals and some larger, family-owned corporations." To some extent, this education process has already started. "There is an increasing awareness of search," suggests Zulueta, "especially among the new generation running family corporations, many of whom have been educated in the United States." One problem is the issue of getting potential clients to understand the professional aspects of search, in a market where the cost of entry is cheap. "Many so-called search firms in the Philippines just accumulate résumés and have thereby given search a bad name."

Zulueta's view is that big search firms will eventually set up in the Philippines, but there is an issue about fees. "If the major search firms stick to fees of 35 per cent of the first year's remuneration, it will be difficult for them to become established here", he argues. "The rates charged by executive search firms in the Philippines can be anything from 10 per cent to 25 per cent, but no one is charging 33.3 per cent or 35 per cent here, as in Hong Kong." Yet it could happen. "Executive search is very competitive in the Philippines", says Orlando Zorilla of accounting firm SGV, with an extensive search and recruitment practice. "It's good if you're successful at the very high level, but there are too many firms in low-level work. Some firms even provide searches for free to very good clients." Yet search in the Philippines is still underdeveloped. "It's nothing like Hong Kong or Singapore", insists Zorilla. "Those places are big time, multinational markets, with many European and American search companies."

EXECUTIVE SEARCH AND SELECTION FIRMS IN THE PHILIPPINES

International Firms

Boyden
W. D. Scott Philippines, Inc. [offices also in Hong Kong (ZMG Bennett Associates), in China (ZMG Bennett Well More) and in Jakarta (HRD)]
SGV/Arthur Andersen
Price Waterhouse

Local Firms

John Clements Consultants, Inc.
Corporate Search Professionals
Garrett Guildford & Associates (a member of Transearch Asia)

There are no major international executive search firms in the Philippines, with the exception of Boyden, represented by Odette Fernandez. But Glendon Rowell from Boyden's Hong Kong operation often flies down to the Philippines to meet with clients and conduct interviews. Fernandez takes care of the research and preliminary interviewing in the Philippines, and then Rowell takes over, from Hong Kong or locally. (A number of other international firms also fly down regularly from Hong Kong, including Spencer Stuart and Korn/Ferry.) W. D. Scott, headed by Zulueta, is a locally-based international company, in so far that the head office is in Manila but branch offices have been set up in Hong Kong and Indonesia. Corporate Search Professionals, run by Philip Gielczyk, is a niche search firm operating only in Manila. Garrett Guildford & Associates, a member of an association of affiliated firms known as Transearch Asia, is a similar operation (principal contact, Stella Guilatko). Accounting firm SGV offers both search and selection, and so does the Philippines' largest recruitment firm, John Clements. Most of these firms offer related consulting services too.

Sectors of Industry in which Firms Specialise

Boyden has a small operation in the Philippines and carries out a few searches per year. The firm has a general practice and, in a typical search, is looking for four private bankers in the Philippines to go to Singapore. The office in Manila thus helps serve other Boyden operations in the region, rather than developing a large domestic business of its own. W. D. Scott's clients are mostly in financial services, consumer goods, and IT. The firm has around fifty clients on a regular basis, most of whom are fast-growing companies. Zulueta gained Citibank as a major client in 1983.

Corporate Search Professionals specialise in CEOs, GMs, and directors of sales and marketing, in a variety of businesses. "Most of the movement of executives in the Philippines is at this level", suggests senior consultant Nanette Dollente. Sixty per cent of their work is in top management, and 40 per cent in middle management. Relying on their database and networking, they do not carry out selection work.

SGV sees itself as probably one of the largest companies in search for financial executives in Manila, recruiting CFOs, treasurers, financial controllers, tax consultants and specialty consultants in the financial arena. It also does some searches for general managers, as well as CEOs, COOs and marketing directors. Most of its work is confined to top functional heads.

Consultant Patty Gallardo of John Clements describes her firm's generalist business: "executive search in the Philippines is not specialised, because the business community is so small, and most of the players are known to each other." Consultants work on different functions, especially in consumer products, pharmaceuticals, trading, chemicals and suppliers of garments.

Average Salary per Assignment

Salaries in the Philippines remain low, although the cost of living is also low. According to the Annual Compensation Survey in the April 1994 issue of *World Executive's Digest,* gross salaries and purchasing power of Philippine managers are the lowest in all management categories. Junior managers in Manila receive just over a quarter of the annual salaries of junior managers in Taipei (US$7,000 compared with US$26,000) and senior managers earn less than half of senior managers in Singapore (US$28,000 compared with US$85,000). Meanwhile, the cost of living index has declined to 70 (against 100 for Hong Kong), leaving Manila as Asia's cheapest city to live in (Tokyo and Taipei are the most expensive).

Search firms concentrate on assignments at the higher end of the salary scale; the lowest salary position searched by W. D. Scott would be half a million pesos, or about US$20,000 per year. Corporate Search Professionals noted that marketing executives are especially in demand, with average annual salaries of around 1.2 million pesos (US$43,000). Middle managers command around US$25,000 p.a. The salaries of the people SGV recruits are around 1 million pesos and upwards (anything below this is not considered as search work). Gallardo of John Clements notes that the top salary for a general manager or CEO is US$100,000 per year maximum. Even very senior jobs command only US$50,000 or US$60,000 a year here, and these are around double the average.

Advice to Aspiring Executives

Glendon Rowell of Boyden reiterates the observation that the most popular companies to work for in the Philippines are the multinationals. He admits that,

> there are not many more setting up here at the moment. The best firms to work for are seen as being Coca-Cola, IBM, and Caterpillar, because the management is very international and they look across the world when they have openings, and often move people internally between different countries. But it's very competitive to get in. I've only exported a few Filipinos so far, but would like to do more. Filipinos are successful overseas, and you can find them speaking any language.

How should you target search firms in the Philippines if you're a Filipino looking for a multinational opening or the chance of an overseas job? Should you send in your résumé or attract headhunters' attention through being well known in your field? Some firms favour both approaches: Zulueta's candidates are selected through industry research and tracking down prominent individuals, and from W. D. Scott's extensive database of write-ins.

Corporate Search Professionals receive fewer write-ins, mostly targeting people through research, but receive many unsolicited résumés from Western expatriates, "although we very rarely bring in expatriates, many approach us, including from the United States", reveals Dollente. She adds,

> Most of them are looking for CEO jobs, but there's not much going, because multinational companies tend to send people out from the head office. It would be better for them to go to search firms in the United States and Hong Kong who place people in the Philippines.

She advises managers to go for a marketing and sales career, which gives a greater chance of getting into general management.

It may seem surprising, but Zorilla of SGV complains of the difficulty of finding executives at the highest levels in the Philippines,

> you can get executives who are not very good, or who are retired, but it's harder to get good ones who are what you want. It can take

one to one and a half months to find these people, excluding the time from when the client agrees to the candidate, to when the candidate is able to join the new company. If we can't find someone in that time, we give up.

High quality executives who are available should take note.

SGV has one of the most international recruitment practices in the Philippines. "We carry out eighty to one hundred search assignments per year, both national and international. These involve moves within the Philippines, and sending people from the Philippines to other places, such as Indonesia, Thailand, and Singapore." Occasionally, Filipinos are also sent to Hong Kong, Taiwan and Malaysia. Some expatriates working in the Philippines have found themselves retrenched, or offered early retirement. Some of these approach SGV and let it be known that they are on the market. "It's almost like outplacement", Zorilla explains. "They come to SGV as individuals and they're helped without charge. But expect benefits once these people are placed." However, only between 5–10 per cent of SGV's searches are for expatriates. The rest are Filipinos. "Expatriates tend to be candidates for regional jobs, such as general manager posts", adds Zorilla. But Filipinos are as good in these jobs as anyone else. "There is a need for Filipinos executives all over Asia because they are more mobile than a number of others. You see Filipinos in executive positions all over the region", he continues.

How should you approach SGV? "We are members of many of the clubs in the Philippines, and the Chambers of Commerce. People can approach our search consultants in these clubs, and mention that they are on the market", Zorilla advises. SGV receives some write-ins, but these are at a top level.

Zorilla explains,

> Generally, people would rather channel their résumé through someone they know, rather than send it in cold. Maybe in the Philippines, it's better to find a mutual friend who knows the headhunter, so they can be contacted through a warm contact as opposed to a cold one.

How Important are Academic Qualifications?

Nanette Dollente of Corporate Search Professionals is typical among search consultants in the Philippines in requiring most candidates to have five to seven years working experience, especially in multinationals. Candidates with tertiary education are highly-regarded, especially graduates of Ateneo, La Salle, and the University of the Philippines (not so much the Asian Institute of Management; many AIM graduates set up their own businesses rather than join companies).

Dollente explains,

> We particularly like people who've been to universities in the United States. This is always a plus, and we especially prefer people who have worked in multinationals because they have the benefits of the training, they have imbued a multinational corporate culture, and they have international standards of working discipline.

Proportion of Expatriate and Local Clients

Multinationals account for about 30 per cent of the volume of executive search firms' work in the Philippines, so there is already a fair proportion of business from local firms: but there is still a long way to go in educating clients, as indicated above. Zuleta feels that "often the client doesn't know what he really wants". Most of the prominent search firms in the Philippines have regional clients too. Zulueta also operates in Hong Kong, Indonesia and Malaysia, and is targeting Vietnam.

Corporate Search Professionals has mostly multinational clients, with some local, but only in the top tier. "We have a small client base, mostly of large companies", insists Dollente.

SGV also has clients all over the region, and Zorilla is coordinating search on a regional basis for the firm. Many executive search leads already emanate from a regional level. SGV's clients are mostly large Filipino conglomerates and multinationals. "It's about fifty/fifty between the two", says Zorilla. "Family businesses are not really involved here; they don't use executive search as such, but carry out their searches through connections." About 20 per cent of SGV's search work is made up of regional assignments. For example, in a search for a general manager for a hotel in Manila, the firm will check out its other offices in other locations in Asia. If they find candidates, the fee is divided between the two offices. Zorilla argues that the percentage of regional business will get larger, possibly to fifty/fifty in two or three years' time.

He said,

> If we want to expand, then we have to go regional, since there is a call for more regional jobs than country managers. Some of the people who were senior managers are now occupying regional posts and there are lots of Filipino expatriates with regional jobs travelling all over Asia.

Proportion of Women among Placements

Zorilla of SGV has found that "ten per cent or less of candidates are women. Human resources is becoming an increasingly popular area for executive search, and many women are recruited at a senior management level in this area, especially for semiconductor companies and firms in the garment trade. A number of women candidates are considered for Chief Financial Officers jobs too", he adds. "Some get shortlisted, but the clients often prefer a man and go so far as to specify this from the outset."

Perceived Competitive Differentiators of Firms

Boyden is clearly in a different league from the other firms, but has only a minor presence. The firm's minimum fee is US$10,000, higher than most other firms in this market. W. D. Scott is one of the most well-known firms in Manila. Originally an Australian-based company, it became established in the Philippines in 1981. At that time it was a management and productivity consultancy, but Zulueta, who bought out the original shareholder, changed the emphasis to search. W. D. Scott employs nine consultants, and nine support staff, and has a separate research unit. The consultants include the ex-human resources director of Digital, the head of human resources at Exxon, and two other ex-human resources personnel from Philippine Airlines and another from IBM. The firm is strongly influenced by Zulueta's urbane and outgoing personality. A graduate of Columbia Business School in New York, he worked previously for both SGV and Peat Marwick. W. D. Scott carries out over 300 searches a year. "I can do search work twice as fast in Manila as in Hong Kong", Zulueta insists. "This is due to my big network of contacts in Manila, and the fact that W. D. Scott's research department is able to put together an extensive initial short list."

Corporate Search Professionals is, by contrast, quite small, with only six staff members. "Only a few choice people know about us", considers Dollente. "We get relatively few unsolicited résumés. We tend to have approached most of the people whose résumés we keep on file." Much networking is carried out through the fact that Philip Gielczyk, the head of the firm, is a member of AmCham in the Philippines. They see themselves as quiet, thorough, discreet and confidential. They charge 25 per cent of the successful candidate's first year's salary, at the high-end of the Philippine market.

Executive search and selection is seen by SGV as a service to its accounting and auditing clients, rather than as a revenue stream in its own way. SGV is the best-known and biggest auditing firm in the Philippines. The executive search arm was set up as an offshoot of the firm's human resources consulting business in 1982. SGV does not aggressively market its search business separately, and 90 per cent of its recruitment work is for existing clients.

Zorilla has been with SGV for twenty-five years. Previously a partner in the Manila office of Arthur Andersen (with whom SGV have a joint arrangement), he is now a partner of the human resources practice in Manila, and spends 20–30 per cent of his time in recruitment. Three people work full-time in executive search and selection for SGV, and Zorilla coordinates the search work being carried out by other people in the firm. With an MBA from Ateneo, and having spent time at the University of Michigan and INSEAD, Zorilla joined SGV when he was half-way though his MBA. He first specialised in organisational restructuring and design, and human resources management, working in Indonesia, Thailand, Pakistan and Sri Lanka. He then handled compensation restructuring and developed the methodology of SGV's executive search. SGV charges 20–25 per cent, according to whether the search is local or international. Many of the consultants used to be clients of the firm, and many of the clients are alumni members of SGV. Zorilla claims that SGV does not have to pitch for assignments,

> because at a higher level, the clients that look at us have already decided to use us. We don't market for business openly, but auditing partners have relationships with clients and introduce them to us. So we basically have a client-base already, which is an advantage in some ways. The disadvantage is that we can't get people from auditing client companies, whereas pure search companies can get them from anywhere that is not a search client.

John Clements, who originated from the Adelaide office of W. D. Scott, set up in the Philippines in 1974, effectively pioneers the search company in the Philippines. John Clements had set up offices in five Australian states before establishing the Philippines office. "We have an image as a management selection company, but actually we have many clients in executive search too. However, this is not marketed in the same way", explains Patty Gallardo, maintaining that the company's business is fifty/fifty search and selection. "We started by developing a low-level management position selection business," she said, "and this opened up more search work for the company." There is a fixed percentage for fees, based on two or three months of the successful candidate's salary.

CLIENT COMMENTS

A major high-tech user comments that,

> Zulueta has been a very impressive research function. As a director of many companies in Manila, he has developed an extensive network of contacts. He takes forty-five days on average for a search,

which we appreciate. In the West, searches can take ninety days, and in Hong Kong, two months is a fair average.

Of Philip Gielczyk, head of the search firm Corporate Search Professionals, and director of the American Chamber of Commerce in the Philippines, one blue-chip Philippine company user commented, "he is a good operator and does very well. It's a niche, specialised business which is very reliable."

One financial user accepts that,

> SGV is quite expensive. For some positions, we pay about half the salary in fees, when the search is based on a time charge, and apparently SGV claims that most of its clients pay on a time-charge basis, especially in searches for CFOs, treasurers, and financial controllers. But since SGV knows these markets very well, and can find good people, it's worth it. We also use them for compensation surveys. Often a company's present compensation structure can indicate why it loses people and has to keep replacing them. We found this was true for us.

ADVERTISED RECRUITMENT/ SELECTION IN THIS MARKET

There are also a number of firms carrying out both search and selection in the Philippines: John Clements, managed by President Leocadio Dominez and Mario Biscocho (Patty Gallardo is another prominent consultant); and accounting firms such as SGV (under Zorilla, who also runs the search business). KPMG Peat Marwick is present in the Philippines but apparently they do not carry out executive recruitment activities; Coopers & Lybrand offered recruitment services in the past but they do not seem to be particularly active in this service any more.

W. D. Scott does some selection work, but does not advertise unless the client insists. If this is the case, advertising is done under their own logo and is never done consecutively. SGV does some advertising, but sees itself as not so aggressive as compared to John Clements or W. D. Scott. Most of the placements made by SGV come out in the Manila Bulletin.

Market leader John Clements probably carries out more than 300 searches a year but, according to industry sources, these are at a lower-level than its competitors (they may even be recruiting secretaries and very junior people). John Clements has been in advertised selection since November 1974, when the firm started.

CHAPTER 11

INDONESIA

Opening Up to Foreign Investment

In this tight market for management talent, especially sought-after executives are doubling and tripling their salaries. Indonesians, Western and Asian expatriates are all cashing in.

With banking deregulation and a host of economic reforms, Indonesia is opening up to foreign investors, and is being flooded by new companies starting up as a result. And the one thing they need most of all is people, and quickly. "There has been some bad recruiting practice as a consequence, with people offered three times their salary", reveals Pri Notowidigdo, partner in executive search firm Tasa in Indonesia. And then, he warns, it has happened that such new start-up companies have gone bust (especially with the Government's tight monetary policy), leaving people on the streets with unrealistically high expectations. Boyden just put a Chinese executive into an expanding Indonesian company, who offered him twice as much money as he was previously earning. Can it last? What will be the effects?

Companies looking to hire executives to work in Indonesia have three choices: they can use local recruitment firms; they can use the branches of international firms, where these exist; and they can carry out long-distance recruiting through hiring firms elsewhere in Asia, but particularly Hong Kong and Singapore. (They are familiar with serving headquarters of multinationals looking to enter the Indonesian market. We don't have detailed information on their activities, but KPMG complained of losing a big search to Spencer Stuart in Hong Kong. These firms send in headhunters on search expeditions, and/or do deals with local firms to represent them.)

An on-the-ground presence by large international search firms in Jakarta is prevented mostly by the generally low fee levels prevalent here, but this could change as the acceptability of search increases. Search is spreading to local companies in Indonesia, but they need to become better educated about how the process works. Search consultants recount stories of sending job descriptions in their proposals to prospective clients, and seeing these being used verbatim in newspaper advertisements without them being given the assignment; of clients disclosing only minimal information to the headhunter, making the job of attracting candidates very difficult; of a client hiring a search firm, then approaching another consultant in the same firm to check up on his colleague; and of clients defaulting on fee payments.

Yet for candidates for jobs in Indonesia, the picture is more straightforward. There is still great potential for expatriates, from the West and the rest of Asia. Ken Japp, who runs his own search business in Jakarta, points out that,

> globalisation of the market-place and the economic downturn in the developed countries has encouraged many domestic managers to seek jobs outside their familiar stamping grounds into foreign lands, such as Indonesia. But unless they're willing to make a conscientious and concerted effort to adapt into the local environment and the method of doing business here, they will find this place very frustrating. Yet, despite all the idiosyncrasies, bureaucracies, etc., things do get done here, and Indonesia, within the Asia Pacific region, is expected to be one of the areas with the most growth prospects in the next ten years.

EXECUTIVE SEARCH FIRMS IN INDONESIA

International Firms

KPMG Hanadi Sudjendro & Rekan
Tasa

Price Waterhouse Konsultan
PT. Sarana Boyden (Boyden International)
Coopers & Lybrand

Local Firms

KBJ ExecuSearch
I.E.S., a division of P. T. Bina Uthana Citra
Eksekutif Search Nusantara

Names of Outstanding Consultants

Of international firms, Pri Notowidigdo of Tasa; Kemal A. Stamboel and Marina R. Tusin of Price Waterhouse Konsultan; W. R. G. King and Dr Sony B. Harsono of Coopers & Lybrand.

Of local firms, Ken Japp of KBJ ExecuSearch; Dan Goldsmith of I.E.S.; Joseph Kaiser of Eksekutif Search Nusantara.

Sectors of Industry in which Firms Specialise

Pri Notowidigdo now with TASA, focuses on senior management and expatriates. Ten per cent of KPMG's clients are industrial conglomerates (these pay substantially higher fees, almost comparable to 90 per cent of the rest). The firm specialises in general manager positions, sales and marketing, and human resources. "Banking and oil are most in demand", Notowidigdo reflects (he was previously with KPMG). "And they're popular, because you get a good training from banks and oil companies, such as Citibank and Total Indonesia. We also do a lot of work in manufacturing and trading." Boyden has also carried out a number of oil company searches. "One of our first assignments was for Mobil oil, looking for attorneys", they explain.

> Banks offer the best money here. We are also working for a French pharmaceutical company. The biggest employers here are textiles and pharmaceuticals. Chinese companies are seen as less attractive by candidates, even if they are also Chinese. There's a perception that only family members make decisions, although the Confucian doctrine of 'you give me your loyalty, and I'll look after you' is widely held.

Ken Japp, with considerable prior experience of search in North America, previously developed a specialism in pharmaceuticals,

> but I also carry out assignments in banking, insurance, TV, consumer products and other areas. There's also a particular

shortage of good people in insurance. It's hard to find people who are good at this, as this industry only came to Indonesia about a decade ago.

Price Waterhouse's work is finance-dominated with recent moves into securities and merchant banking. "These organisations are showing great demand for recruiting junior people to be trained as financial analysts", explains Kemal A. Stamboel.

> Previously, this gap was being filled by experts from Hong Kong and Singapore. It takes time to get expertise developed here for the organisations which need it. On the manufacturing side, whilst the economy is quite active, there is not so much movement among top people, such as plant managers and general managers. Most of the mobility is in marketing and finance.

Of functional areas in big demand, Stamboel points to the importance of the human resources function: "some think this is an easy area, but it's a most complex job, and only top management really understand the need. They drive the human resources role in the organisation, differentiating it from personnel, which is steps below." Coopers & Lybrand also focus on the financial side. They undertake some search, but mostly selection.

Average Salary per Assignment

Salary levels in Indonesia are traditionally on the middle to lowside in the context of Asia as a whole: usually above the Philippines and Thailand, but below Singapore, Hong Kong and Taiwan. Junior managers get only one-sixth of Asia's highest salary, and middle managers only a quarter. Senior and top managers are paid around the lower end of the Asian league table, getting around US$50,000 p.a.. In terms of purchasing power, Indonesia-based executives have a clear advantage, and top managers here are better off than their counterparts in many locations, including Taiwan. The cost of living in Indonesia remains among the lowest in Asia, just ahead of Malaysia and the Philippines. However, expatriates are warned that everyone has to pay three years' rent up-front, around US$4,000 a month for a large home in the suburbs.

Judging by salaries, manufacturing and engineering talent is in most demand, where salaries are on par with Hong Kong and Korea. Purchasing and logistics executives in Indonesia are paid more than anywhere else in the region. Personnel managers are paid only marginally less than in Hong Kong, although Singapore and Taiwan are out in front here. EDP managers are running just behind Hong Kong and

Singapore. Financial executives in Indonesia get more than in Thailand, the Philippines and Korea. Sales and marketing executives' salaries, however, are still lagging behind.

KPMG handle assignments with wide-ranging salaries, typically starting at US$10,000 a month for expatriates, and US$6,000 a month for Indonesians. General Managers get US$2,000 to US$7,000 (this includes tax of around 30 per cent). Many successful candidates receive thirteen months' salary, especially in banks and oil companies. Cars are expensive in Indonesia – three to four times as expensive as in the United States – so they are seen as a significant perk in managerial packages (a Honda Accord, costing US$16,000 in the United States, will cost US$45,000–50,000 in Indonesia, and a US$45,000 Mercedes will be priced at US$125,000 here). Houses are also expensive, and banks charge high interest rates. You can borrow money more cheaply if you work for a bank, so this is an important consideration. "Indonesians now especially want to work for international companies", Notowidigdo considers. "There's a general belief that they pay more money." Ken Japp handles assignments at salary levels up to US$250,000 p.a., and also some lower-level work when required by existing clients, mostly for multinationals.

Stamboel of Price Waterhouse, with his primary interest in financial positions, sees banks as encouraging executive mobility in Indonesia. The demand for executives by banks has led to the escalation of salaries in banking, and some local executives in this field have achieved parity with multinational executives, "not across the board but in some particular areas." Price Waterhouse search and selection assignments are for positions with salaries from US$2,000 a month, with the highest from US$12,000–14,000. The minimum for search would be US$5,000–7,000 per month.

Advice to Aspiring Executives

There is still some unfamiliarity with being headhunted in Indonesia. "Still people feel uneasy, but there are techniques for approaching them so they don't feel hunted", explains Notowidigdo.

> We call people as sources but really we want them as candidates, but this is better than approaching them direct. It means we can test the situation first, and we also ask someone who's close to a person to ascertain how interested he or she might be. But don't assume that sourcing calls are actually invitations to be considered as a candidate.

Many people are leaving medium-sized Indonesian companies for multinationals and large Indonesian conglomerates, but they should make it clear that it's not just for the more generous packages. "Big conglomerates demand accountability", continues Notowidigdo. "People come to a stage in their careers when they want more power, not just money, and they can get this in an Indonesian conglomerate, such as Rajawali." They must be ready to embrace this increased responsibility.

As we've seen, Indonesia is increasingly popular among expatriates. But you should do your homework first, warns Ken Japp. "I was recently involved with expatriate candidates who had never been to Indonesia. I made a special effort to explain what it is like to work here." White of Boyden also sees lots of expatriates, but insists that it's hard for them to get a job if they expect very high salaries. Stamboel has to overcome arguments that Indonesia is categorised as politically of high-risk, but suggests it is safe, and has a stable government.

Many want to go into the financial sector, which is growing most quickly in Indonesia, but those targeting a job in Indonesia from outside or inside should also consider manufacturing. This is also big, but is attracting different people. Manufacturing means big business for recruiters now, with a higher quantity of work (although the financial area is attracting higher salaries).

Stamboel warns employers in Indonesia to avoid job-hoppers.

> It's not acceptable to change jobs too often, especially if it means not moving up the ladder. It doesn't look good to move every year or two but keep to the same level. The job market is becoming more mobile, but people look at the stableness of people, and their dedication to their company is important. Moving every two years approximately for a clear promotion opportunity is more acceptable.

How Important are Academic Qualifications?

Experience is ranked far ahead of academic qualifications here, as practical knowledge of the job is seen as paramount. Of MBAs, those from overseas are more sought-after. Stamboel's candidates include many who are foreign educated.

> Some local MBAs fit in well with international standards, but lots are unknown internally. We don't see having an MBA as an important criteria for appointment. We still have to go through the analysis of where the person is from. But we do look for good MBAs from more recognised institutions, such as those run by state-owned universities or with links with universities abroad (like Harvard and Stanford). But even with this, it doesn't mean everyone has the same standard.

In Indonesia, experience with multinationals is rated just as highly as academic qualifications. The Indonesian Lippo Group hires many staff from multinationals known for their excellent training programmes, such as Citibank.

Proportion of Expatriate and Local Clients

KPMG's clients are 90 per cent multinationals, but they are trying to build up their local clientele. They are harder to work for, however: "you have to tell Indonesians that you need time to handle the search properly, even though they want someone yesterday. We have a manual of search practice, and stick to it for all clients." Price Waterhouse's clients also include multinationals and local companies:

> most multinationals normally use professional recruiters, and local companies are starting to use search too, but many local companies feel they have their own local knowledge and networks and can do search on their own, and this belief is preventing us from doing more business with them.

Proportion of Women among Placements

KPMG note that women candidates are increasing in number, and not just in human resource roles. Marketing and finance are popular areas for women, and accounting firms want more women accountants. They are seen as having a greater eye for details, as being more trustworthy, and more loyal. Boyden see lots of women candidates: "Some are very good." Price Waterhouse see more women candidates than men. There is only one male out of twelve consultants on the firm's finance side. This is not a deliberate preference, Stamboel suggests, but only women candidates pass the standard. "They're getting into more senior positions, and moving up quickly. It's not such a big deal." The management shortages in Indonesia are certainly giving women more breaks.

Looking towards Other Countries as Sources of Candidates

Generally, Malaysia discourages expatriates, Singapore tolerates them, but in Indonesia, employers *want* expatriates. KPMG's candidates include a mix of Filipinos and Indians. "We place a lot of them at double their salaries", reveals Notowidigdo.

> We placed an Indian as senior VP with American Express, at double what he was earning before. Of all our candidates, 70 per cent are Indonesians, and the rest are expatriates. Some Indonesians are

expatriates too, they've been away and are now coming back, mostly as Americans. Of our Western expatriates, the most popular group are Americans, British, and Australians. Indians and Filipinos come here in large numbers, but it can be hard to place them if they expect too much. Overall, the gap is narrowing between salaries of expatriates and locals, but expatriates are still higher-paid, and employers still pay less if they hire an Indonesian.

He warns that costs are higher for expatriates, which is helping in the levelling out process (school fees are much less for locals).

Ken Japp has orchestrated a number of candidate travels from Australia, Hong Kong, Singapore and the Philippines to meet with clients in Jakarta. "Because of the rapid economic developments in this country and the shortage of qualified managers, especially in areas which are new to Indonesia, we are relying heavily on outside expertise", he points out. "Many of these people would come in on a two to three year contract which is renewable thereafter on a yearly basis."

Perceived Competitive Differentiators of Firms

There are relatively few search firms in Indonesia, and they are dominated by the key individuals running them, so their personalities are the most obvious competitive differentiator.

Tasa's Notowidigdo, having travelled extensively through his work on the Canadian aid programme, is a very international Indonesian. He's very active in the community, offering forty hours a year of free consultation at IPMI. He writes two monthly columns in *SWA*, a local magazine modelled on *Fortune* and connected with *Tempo*.

In June 1987, Notowidigdo set up KPMG executive search, having been with Price Waterhouse before, and was made partner very quickly. "We have grown rapidly in this market. We made US$120,000 in our first year, by end of 1988, which was then doubled to US$250,000 in the following year", he explains. "We then reached US$420,000, and last year was US$720,000. The search business has now levelled off, and revenues are not doubling every year any more. We now offer three areas of expertise: executive search; compensation consulting; and organisation and development." The firm aims to keep the search business this size, with two consultants. Notowidigdo has a very practical way of working which might shock search purists in the West. Active candidates are listed on data storage cards (350 entries on each card) which he carries with him to show to clients when making proposals. He joined Tasa in mid-1994.

Ken Japp (who concentrates more on executive search as opposed to selection than anyone else in this market) started in search more than ten years ago in North America. From a career with Hoffmann La-Roche in sales and marketing, he operated an executive search practice in Canada for eight years before returning to Indonesia to enter his family business. Over the last four years he's been active in search in Indonesia, specialising in search for positions paying salaries of US$100,000 and above, and charges 33.3 per cent (most other firms here work for lower fees). Japp, who operates as a one-man-band, argues that he offers significant advantages over firms which are not located here. "It's hard to carry out effective networking if you only visit this place occasionally", he insists.

> I organised a golf tournament here – producing a good mix of people, some clients, some not – which was useful for networking purposes. My clients are mostly multinationals, but I've been developing Indonesian companies as clients too. My candidates are mostly Indonesians, and the majority of them are from multinationals. My searches take one month on average. I find it harder to do lots of searches at one time here than in Canada, where I often did six or seven at a time. Here, it's harder to find qualified candidates and telecommunications and travel is less efficient.

It can be more efficient for multinational search firms trying to operate here to have a representative on the spot. Boyden is one of the international branded search firms operating in Jakarta (Tasa is another, and in the future Amrop may formalise their representation). Boyden in Indonesia gained support from David Keith in Singapore, and has now been operating for nearly two years. "We have some good people on our books whom we market to companies", they explain. "Our candidates are mostly Indonesians, with a few expatriates. We can complete some searches very quickly: we did one in two weeks. We'd prefer to work for fewer clients, offering salary survey advice, for example."

Price Waterhouse's recruitment activity, handled by twelve consultants, ranges from eighty to one hundred positions a month, with 10–15 per cent of assignments carried out by search. They've been in Jakarta a long time. "Twenty years ago, our management consulting practice was established," Stamboel explains, "and in 1979, we started recruiting. We now have finance and HR divisions, IT, business strategy, marketing and finance systems and organisation research." The HR area carries out training and organisational work, but "executive search and selection is our bread and butter", considers Stamboel. "We charge 20–25 per cent on recruitment, which can go to 30 per cent on the search side, or we can agree a fixed fee. But even 20–25 per cent is hard for most firms to get here. Our reputation allows us to charge as much as we do."

CLIENT COMMENTS

One client in the financial services sector points out,

> The name KPMG is a big door-opener, because the firm is so well known. We can trust their confidentiality, and the reputation of the firm certainly pulls in good candidates. You could probably say the same for Price Waterhouse.

According to one extensive search user,

> In terms of ranking firms in the market here, KPMG and Price Waterhouse are about the same. Possibly the latter may be making more revenues as it has more people, but they charge 18–20 per cent, but KPMG charges 25 per cent and more for higher level search, whilst Ken Japp charges 33.3 per cent, as he handles mostly top-level searches only. Korn/Ferry are doing some work here. They come every two to three months, for a week, and have no indigenous business. They're just serving clients out of Singapore and Hong Kong. Egon Zehnder are about the same. Spencer Stuart and Russell Reynolds come here about once a year, and seem to be less active, but it's hard to say exactly. W. D. Scott from the Philippines work on assignments here from time to time. Amrop, through Tan Soo Jin from Singapore, are fairly active here, and Tasa also search here often, now having set up an office in Indonesia.

"Price Waterhouse must be the biggest recruitment office in town but, like most of the others, they're doing more selection than search", considers a leading user of recruitment services in the banking sector.

RECRUITMENT/SELECTION FIRMS IN INDONESIA

International Firms

KPMG Hanadi Sudjendro & Rekan
Price Waterhouse Konsultan
SGV (across the Asia region, link with Arthur Andersen)
Coopers & Lybrand

Local Firms

TSP & Associates (Tommy S. Praptasuganda and Nerissa S. Reyes)

PAP (a spin-off from PA)
I.Q. Recruitment & Training Specialists (part of Quatro)

The selection business in Indonesia is relatively well developed, and recruitment ads pull well here. "When KPMG had an assignment for Sempati Air, we had 7,000 applicants for one advertisement", reveals Notowidigdo. When KPMG wants to offer lower-level recruitment services, clients are referred to TSP, with whom KPMG has a strategic alliance. If KPMG is given a job to look for engineers, they would do a file search on their database only, or pass it directly to TSP. Other selection firms include PAP (a spin-off from a former PA operation) which is run by two Filipinos, and Quatro. SGV are also involved in recruitment, but they're not looking to expand into this area, and reports suggest that they are pulling out here. 85–90 per cent of Price Waterhouse's assignments are for selection, which are advertised under their own name (about 50 per cent of these are in the financial area).

TSP – founded in September 1990 – exchange candidates with KPMG and serve clients together. They're working towards creating the same database format. Tommy Praptasuganda, originally from Arthur Andersen's tax division, claims that his methodology and approach is the same as KPMG's. TSP's salary level starts at US$30,000 p.a.

He claims that:

> There are requirements here for auditors, junior bankers and analysts in particular. The overheads are high for KPMG, so they have to stay at the top levels, and give smaller scale work to others. We can meet objectives together by dividing territories and, at the end of the day, the client is served according to his needs. About 10 per cent of our work and two to three clients are connected with KPMG, but through these clients, we get valuable other clients. More than half of our clients have Euro/US link ups, especially oil, gas and mining (joint-ventures with Exxon, Arco, Vico, and mining companies, Freeport and ABB). About 35 per cent of our work involves searching our database, and the rest is advertising. There are many mergers and acquisitions going on in Indonesia, so we are doing lots of outplacement work, around 10 per cent of our business. We have another alliance to find Filipino candidates. 15–20 per cent of our candidates are Filipinos, and the rest are locals.

The average salaries handled by TSP are US$5,000 a month for managers, and the lowest is US$15,000 a month, at supervisory level. They have a special interest in finance and accounting people, either SGV or AA graduates. Praptasuganda describes the situation,

It's still rare to get good accountants in Indonesia. We don't produce as many good accountants to meet the demand. SGV graduates a minimum of 200 a year and recruits at least another 200 a year. We started with accountants, and now we are building up a datafile on engineers, real estate and property executives. Office space is booming right now. We meet many people who write in. They can be hot merchandise, so we talk to them and ask our clients if they need them. We have equal numbers of male and female candidates on our database, with the females particularly into accounting, finance and IT. We're looking for technical requirements, leadership qualities and good English. We don't put a premium on local MBAs. Most of them don't meet US standards.

TSP's revenues are growing at 100 per cent p.a., and they expect this to continue for the next two to three years, and then to carry on at around 50 per cent p.a.. Revenues are currently US$700,000 with twenty-two people, in a range of human resources consulting and training activities as well as recruitment. Praptasuganda emphasizes that with a growing market in Indonesia, professionals move a lot. Because there are few places companies can tap, two to three years is seen as long enough with one company, at the middle management level. "There's more mobility now in the job market, especially with the bank boom which started two years ago, and the current boom in property and construction. Many industries here are not mature, and there's an ongoing need for expatriates."

Price Waterhouse's advertised recruitment business covers the salary range of US$2,000–6,000 a month, and they advertise for around sixty-five to eighty-five positions a month (although some of these may be filled through the firm's database. At least 60 per cent are successful placements, and take between two weeks to one and a half months to complete. Sometimes they will advertise regionally, and will ask the local Price Waterhouse office in those cities to undertake the necessary interviewing. The greatest areas of shortage noted by Price Waterhouse's selection side are in human resources, marketing and finance.

PART THREE

THE EXECUTIVE
SEARCH PROCESS

CHAPTER 12

EXAMINING THE SEARCH PROCESS

OVERVIEW

To cut through the mystique surrounding the search process, we need a systematic examination of every stage to evaluate how an assignment is handled, to see how the headhunting process itself actually works.

This begins with the first contact between the headhunter and the client – or would-be client – at the briefing stage, at which the whole problem of the position to be filled is first raised. How should the client prepare for this meeting, and what questions will a headhunter ask? In many cases, the headhunter at this stage will be competing against rival search firms for the job. The presentation will therefore be concerned not merely with the client's recruitment problem, but why the client should choose that particular consultant and search firm. Sometimes the client will decide then and there, immediately after the shoot-out or competitive pitch for the assignment at his or her office. On other occasions, especially in the case of a subsidiary or branch of a large multinational, each search firm pitching for the assignment will subsequently write letters to the client discussing the appointment and describing their own particular credentials for the task. How should the client choose between them? Once a headhunter has been engaged, what initial enquiries should then be made before the search begins?

Back at the search firm's offices, what happens when the assignment is turned over to the research department? Which methods are used to narrow down the field of candidates? Each firm has a slightly different approach to the research phase, both in the variety of sources – formal and informal – and in the role the researcher plays in the assignment as a whole. What are the quickest and most effective research techniques? What is the nature of the relationship between the researcher and the consultant? Who makes the telephone call?

What happens when the would-be candidates are interviewed by the headhunter? What should both parties be looking for? How does the search consultant set about fleshing out the bones of a CV or résumé when he or she meets the subject face-to-face? How does the headhunter use information from the interview to report back to the client? And what might a candidate expect when faced with psychometric testing? How frequently do clients, and search firms, insist on it? What is its value in the selection process?

The final decision of which candidate to appoint rests with the client, but on the basis of what sort of information, and how much time with the candidates? What part does the headhunter play in the final negotiations? What happens afterwards: should the search consultant keep in touch with both the successful candidate and (presumably) satisfied client?

What happens if it all goes wrong and the company subsequently feels unhappy with the new appointee, or the expertly headhunted individual is just as expertly headhunted by someone else soon afterwards, or decides that he or she does not actually like the new position after all? What form of guarantees do headhunters make, and what is their after-sales service like?

So what happens first when a company has a senior vacancy to fill? At what stage would a headhunter be called in? Not immediately, unless the company is one which has used executive search in the past. By the time he is asked to start work, two events may have taken place. First, an executive may have left unexpectedly, and an attempt to find an internal replacement has failed; or, second, adequate thought has not been given to the question of succession, and an important director is rapidly approaching retirement, while the executive assumed to accept promotion to this position has other plans. Generally, but not always, there is a high degree of urgency involved and most clients would agree that this would be likely to increase once the company has tried and failed to handle the problem itself.

Does the client then inform the search firm about the nature of the requirement, or do the two meet to discuss the problem? Headhunters would always take one of their colleagues to the client briefing with them to ensure continuity if for any reason they were unable to carry on with the search. Many headhunters would expect to discuss the circumstances surrounding the requirement with the client and the successful candidate's future colleague in some detail and what was needed would be decided together before defining the actual position to be filled. The questions which the headhunter would particularly ask would first concern how confidential the search process was to be. Then he would need to know the nature of the management and corporate structure of the company and how the new executive is to fit into that structure; how senior the position to be filled is, what the reporting lines and the key responsibilities of the individual to be recruited are, and what qualifications are needed.

This information would enable the headhunter to draw up a two-dimensional specification: details of the position which can be agreed in writing. Of more interest from his point of view, however, is the third dimension, which cannot be so easily put into words: what sort of executive fits this company? What important criteria does the particular company have that is unique to that company and reflects the personality of its leaders and culture? What solution might be acceptable, and what proposals would it absolutely refuse to consider? For example, would they or would they not employ a woman? To what level of responsibility could the person they are looking for ultimately aspire or, in other words, what is the upward potential of the job? Is there anyone in the company who already feels that he or she is in line for the job, and will they be disappointed if an outsider is appointed instead?

Who is going to be involved with managing the search project from the client end, and who is going to be on the jury to choose between the candidates at the short list stage?

The successful candidate does not by any means always come from outside the company. Many clients argue that before moving to the stage of appointing a search firm, the personnel director should have already exhausted the possibilities within the company; in view of the ultimate cost of involvement with a headhunter, sensibly the company should have already carried out the process of checking its own people thoroughly. Many clients see the role of the headhunter as coming in then, and penetrating beneath the surface of the problem. This is a much greater task than seeking an executive to fill the post from outside, for the headhunter may well discover that there is someone inside the company who is ideally suited and whom the client has not noticed. This can easily happen in the case of a large company with diversified subsidiaries, a large global trading company or any major business with overseas operations. It has often been known for an individual somewhere to be overlooked, who subsequently turns out to be the ideal person for the position to be filled.

Sometimes, after the client briefing, the headhunter and client together find that there isn't actually a job to be filled after all. At the briefing stage, often before the headhunter has agreed to undertake the assignment and before the client has officially appointed him or her, they may both agree that there is no need for outside search at all. In this case what the client actually requires is reassurance that internal executives measure up well against the competition that may exist in the market-place generally, and that in reality the headhunter has been called on to supply a second opinion. Many headhunters would not wish to start work on an assignment unless they can be sure that there was 'a desire to hire' on the part of the client.

Once the specification of the type of executive required had been agreed, how would the headhunter approach the task of pin-pointing the individual? Would he or she already have a mental picture of the list of people he or she might approach, or be starting from scratch? Before beginning work on the search, many headhunters – in the case of a senior level search for a client they wished to develop a good future relationship with – would ask to visit the place where the executive to be appointed would work and, if the company were involved in manufacturing, to have seen at least some of the factories and workshops. Sometimes, if the search was not too confidential, a headhunter might ask to meet the colleagues with whom the new executive would work, to understand how he or she would fit into the organisation, even to the extent of seeing the chair and desk which would be occupied. Clients often think this is essential for the headhunter to fully grasp all the dimensions of the problem.

Headhunters often maintain that only very rarely have they had to start a search from scratch. If the position is a general management appointment, it is very likely that they or their firm will have direct experience of working in the same industry. An executive search firm in business for a number of years will have completed literally thousands of search assignments, so there would already be an extensive residue of contacts in their data base, as candidates and as sources of referrals to candidates.

The headhunter would also expect to discuss with clients their competitors and the executives in those companies whom they most admire. Most clients have a view of who their competition are, and this helps the headhunter to focus on the field of candidates and where he or she is most likely to find them.

But does this mean that headhunting is to some extent poaching? In that when an executive is moved, he or she is inevitably denuding one place to add to another. The charge of poaching is valid, it is a fact of life in headhunting. But for an executive to be poached may be seen as a back-handed compliment to a company; it reflects the organisation's success in training and management development. There are strict rules about poaching in headhunting, especially relating to previous and existing clients. Poaching from one's clients is like a little boy building a tower of bricks and trying to remove bricks from underneath while at the same time putting them on the top. In best practice, an executive whom a search consultant has recruited would not subsequently be contacted for another opportunity, at least not for several years, and when the company was no longer a client. This code of conduct – practised by the leading firms but not necessarily strictly adhered to by all – naturally limits the number of clients in one sector of any search firm. Paradoxically, too many clients can sometimes be bad for business in the executive search world.

In eyeing up the client company's competition so that he or she can find suitable candidates for the job, how does the consultant go about making the initial approach? Ideally, the headhunter has to know as much as possible about the executive before calling them. Telephone calls to candidates from search consultants can, of course, vary enormously in quality, from headhunters who do their research properly to those who know nothing at all about the person they are calling and end up causing considerable embarrassment. Senior staff in multinational companies in particular are used to receiving calls from headhunters, and soon realise whether or not the consultant has really done the necessary homework and found out much about them before telephoning.

One of the headhunter's greatest problems is that the people whom he or she is phoning are, by definition – otherwise they should not be phoning them in the first place – successful, hard-working and busy, invariably too busy to look through newspapers for job advertisements and never having much time for long telephone conversations. So the search consultant has to put across, as the representative of the client, in a short period of time during the first brief telephone call exactly what the problem is and who is needed to solve it. The headhunter has to impart this information in such a way that it is going to attract the attention of the individual and arouse his or her curiosity enough to set up an initial meeting. No headhunter can adequately interview important potential candidates over the telephone, so most calls are made with the view of setting up a meeting somewhere, often at the headhunter's office.

The headhunter's problems in making such telephone calls especially to candidates working in financial institutions – are compounded by the fact that many telephone conversations received by these concerns are taped as a matter of policy. Several finance houses keep records of the conversations held across their telephone lines. If a search consultant is telephoning the treasurer of a bank, for example, and the call has been taped and heard by the latter's superior, this would cause great problems for the consultant's client, probably another bank trying to headhunt that treasurer. So, in these cases, the headhunter has to try to interest the candidate in the position with the minimum of information, and ask that the conversation be continued, possibly when the latter is at home later that evening. This problem of the recording of incoming telephone calls is not, of course, encountered across the board in business, but it emphasizes the discretion with which a headhunter must always work. Discretion is one of the most vital attributes of a successful search consultant: every day, people are going to impart many confidential items of information, things about themselves which should never be repeated without their express permission.

When the headhunter does finally come up with someone who seems to be the ideal person for the job, inevitably the client – left to make the final decision – does not always agree; but in the majority of cases, if the headhunter has done his homework and has worked closely with the client all along, the problem will be resolved satisfactorily and the position filled. In any case, it is not a question of the client either accepting or rejecting one candidate. It is the headhunter's job to present a group of candidates – four, five, six, or even seven or eight – after having weeded out many more who are deemed unsuitable. Those who never reached this stage could well have been highly competent on technical and professional grounds, but not suitable in terms of the totality of the problem.

The final, most suitable candidates are presented to the client first by report and then physically by interview, in a sufficiently short period of time such that when the client sees the fifth candidate, he or she can still remember what the first one was like. The headhunter can help the client manage the interviewing process by acting as an intermediary in the delicate salary negotiations and by carrying out extensive reference checking on the chosen candidate before the person is actually hired.

Could this solution have been achieved by advertising, especially in view of the high charges imposed by most headhunting firms? Arguably (as discussed in Chapter 3) advertising can be just as expensive: advertisements go to the world, and that is why one pays so much for them. But the client only wants one executive in the end, and the odds are that the person has not even seen the advertisement, let alone applied for the post. Advertising offers no guarantee of success and for

134

appointments paying over a certain amount (varying over the region), many clients prefer to use search.

If, and this is increasingly the case, top jobs are not advertised, does this encourage an élitism in business which is very hard for up-and-coming executives to break into? Both headhunters and clients agree that this is to some extent true, but welcome such élitism. After all, they argue, here we are discussing executives who are going to have a tremendous influence on all aspects of the business they enter, so they must be among the élite and a member of the élite tailored for the specific job in mind.

Also, the personnel director or other executive responsible for the search is putting his or her reputation on the line just as much as the headhunter. In seeking to fill an especially crucial position, in 'looking for someone who can make things happen, to be a lamp around which moths will fly', the client and the consultant both have a great deal at stake. And what is the success rate? Some firms have a high-level of repeat business, between 60–80 per cent, which is a considerable achievement in the world of business generally, where memories are short on success and long on failure.

THE BRIEF

When the new client (C) first telephones the headhunter, C may indicate simply the title of the position which needs to be filled. C will then ask the headhunter to visit him or her at the client's premises or, for reasons of confidentiality, may request a meeting in the headhunter's office. At this very early stage, the consultant should ask C to prepare for the initial meeting. The headhunter will ask C to come to the meeting with an organisation chart, indicating where the job fits and to whom the person will report. The consultant should also ask C to prepare an initial job specification, and also to give some thought to the type of person C wants to hire, and the parameters of the compensation package which the company is prepared to offer. It is a good discipline for C to have to write at least something down on paper before the first meeting with the headhunter.

When the first meeting takes place, the headhunter will want to know something about the history and culture of the organisation, and also what has happened to create the vacancy which is to be filled. Is the previous job holder retiring; did he or she leave; or were they fired? If it was not a simple question of retirement, then the consultant needs to know why the previous incumbent went, because this is one of the first questions which potential candidates will ask of the headhunter. The headhunter will then want to know C's views on the preferred age of the person, who will do the interviewing of the final candidates, what sort of qualifications the candidates need to have, and what sort of job experience would be most desirable. The consultant also needs to know any organisations which are off-limits for the search, and C should also establish with the headhunter which companies are off-limits to the search firm.

The briefing to the consultant should be carried out by the immediate superior of the person to be hired. He or she is the ultimate decision maker, and the only one who really knows what qualities and what type of person is needed. It is often useful to have the personnel director or head of human resources at this initial meeting, because in many cases the chairman or chief executive does not find it easy to express or verbalise a description of the culture of the organisation. Furthermore, many chairmen and senior directors may not know much about the details of the normal fringe benefits which the company offers to senior executives.

The headhunter should leave this initial meeting with a clear understanding of why C wishes to recruit somebody to fill the job, and what sort of person is needed to be the ideal candidate. When the consultant returns to the firm's office, the next task is to prepare a draft of the job specification which describes C's organisation, the responsibilities and reporting structure of the job to be filled, the qualifications, age, etc. of the ideal candidate, and a clear indication of the principal features of the compensation package which will be offered, i.e. whether there is a bonus and/or stock options in addition to salary.

The headhunter now submits a letter to C – four examples of which are discussed next – which sets out the proposed methodology of the search, the fees which will be charged, and the draft specification. The consultant should very clearly request that C read the job specification carefully and amend or correct it as necessary. This is vital to ensure that C is clear at the outset on the sort of person he or she wants to hire, and the headhunter has a shared understanding of the detailed objectives of the search. The more difficult and less effective clients do not bother to read the job specification properly and thus can cause themselves and the headhunter considerable pain later on in the search. The best clients read the job specification very carefully and make precise and detailed corrections and amendments in order to make sure that the job specification is drawn clearly and succinctly.

Finally, before starting the search, but when confirmation that the headhunter has won the assignment has been received, a visit to C's principal office or location is absolutely vital. In some cases secrecy prevents the headhunter from making this visit – for example, when a replacement for an existing executive is being sought, whilst the present incumbent is still installed – but, when at all possible, the headhunter should seek to spend at least a day visiting the plant and offices of his new client, and meeting as many of the key directors and senior management of the organisation as possible. Only in this way will the consultant develop a feel for the culture and environment into which the new recruit will be introduced. The headhunter will also gain from this visit a picture and understanding of C. This is not only valuable in pointing likely candidates, but also enables the consultant to speak with much more authority to potential candidates about their client. There is nothing worse than a headhunter who seems to know very little about the client for whom the search is being undertaken. Conversely, there is nothing more impressive than a headhunter who is able to answer any questions that potential candidates care to throw at him.

So, what should the client employing the headhunter look for in the initial brief? On what grounds should the choice be made? Frequently, the successful search consultant is simply the one with whom the client feels most comfortable as, after all, they will have to be able to work together closely. But a lot of money is at stake here, and the winning firm should clearly be highly professional, experienced and willing to put its cards on the table. As far as the user of search is concerned, the headhunting firm should:

1. Present a brief and clear understanding of the problem, and state when the work could begin;

2. Set out the search firm's methods and approach in a precise, competent and relevant manner. Clients should be wary of potentially dangerous short cuts;

3. Have taken some time and trouble with the proposal, and indicated that the firm was willing to become very closely involved with the client's problem, as opposed merely to setting its headhunting wheels in motion with a standardised, ready-made solution;

4. Set out a time scale for the search programme. Too brief an estimate looks suspicious: has the headhunter really understood the problem?;

5. Provide a clear and perceptive profile of the ideal candidate. Are any specific search and recruiting problems envisaged at this stage?;

6. Make a clear statement of the firm's charges. Is this based on one-third of the successful candidate's salary, or is it a professional fee? This can have a bearing on the attitude of the headhunter to the search, as it suggests it is in the consultant's interest that the appointee is paid as much as possible, when this can hardly be to the client's advantage. The client will normally want to keep the search budget as low as possible, or is the importance of the

assignment such that this consideration is relatively insignificant? Is there any kind of guarantee, in the event of dissatisfaction on the part of the client, that the search would be continued for expenses only after a certain period had elapsed?;

7. Estimate the overall total cost of the search and placement, including expenses. Some headhunters have been known almost to double their total bill with expenses charges. The client should expect an estimate of these, and insist on prior approval being sought for all large individual expense items, such as intercontinental flights and lengthy overseas phone calls;

8. Describe in detail the credentials of the headhunting consultants who will take on the job. If the client wants the man or woman present at the shoot-out to take on the assignment, then this should be insisted upon at the outset, otherwise it could very well be handled by a less experienced and less able lower-ranking associate with more time at his or her disposal. Clients should be wary of firms where the MD does the selling and the other consultants, kept in the background, do the work. Have the consultants who are poised to take on the assignment had the necessary experience to understand the ramifications of the position to be filled, by having worked in a similar company, having carried out a closely-related function, and having helped to solve many other search assignments of a similar nature? Does the consultant possess the technical and linguistic ability to take on the specific assignment? Certain consultants have gained a reputation for expertise in specific areas; the client should seek the views of personnel and executive colleagues in their own and other firms, especially when taking on a new headhunting firm for the first time;

9. Reiterate the importance of confidentiality and be willing to commit themselves to it absolutely;

10. Ask the client what companies the search firm should not use as hunting grounds from the client's point of view, and the consultant should give a clear idea which companies are off-limits to the headhunting firms. Should the headhunter reveal the names of existing clients in this regard? Would this break their confidentiality agreements?

Finally, if the client, after the shoot-out, feels that a close enough relationship had been developed with a particular headhunter to justify the latter signing off a brief with the words 'warmest personal regards', then they should consider engaging that firm. If not, they would do well to be wary. It is better to be businesslike than over friendly until a real *modus operandi* has been established and the search is showing good progress or has been successfully completed.

RESEARCH

In the overall strategy to draw up a short list of candidates for the client, the search element is arguably most important of all. Most assignments spend more time in the hands of a headhunter's research department than any other stage of the headhunting process, except perhaps during the time that the successful candidate is working out his or her notice; and if the client is not happy with the short list, then it is back to the drawing board and the assignment will be turned over to the researcher again. Before consultants can begin work on screening and sifting through the first trawl of potential candidates to get to the initial lengthy short list, they are entirely dependent upon the researcher's input.

Yet, despite all these considerations, the research aspect of search is the one most shrouded in mystery from the client's point of view. Most users of search, however experienced and knowledgeable, know almost nothing about what happens at the research stage and the skills needed for this job. It has indeed proved difficult here to obtain a clear picture of exactly what happens when the assignment 'goes to the research department'.

Many headhunters' researchers complain that their consultant bosses do not understand their jobs, and as a result they lack encouragement and adequate technical support. Research undertaken for this book shows, firstly, that the differing attitudes to research by headhunting firms is one of the principal differences between them, and research capability is a useful criteria of their professionalism; and secondly, that headhunting research is immensely skilled and hard work and, once clients realise what is involved, most of them are more appreciative of what they get for their money. Increasingly efficient research systems and methods are helping to make headhunting more cost-effective for lower-level searches, so good researchers are thus encouraging further growth of the headhunting industry as a whole.

Headhunting Research: Myths and Reality

To what extent is new research undertaken for each particular headhunting assignment, and how reliant is the researcher on the existing candidate and source documentation already available from the search firm's databank, amassed from previous assignments, coded and stored? Possibly the most widespread – and certainly the most inaccurate – myth of the headhunting business is that headhunters' candidates all spring magically from their databanks, and thus clients prefer to go to the largest and most long-established search firms because these have the most extensive files. There is some evidence that many users of search think that this is wholly or at least partly the case.

Representations and descriptions of search in the media have encouraged belief in the myth that candidates' names merely pop out of a computer. In reality, in the case of most professional, senior level executive search firms, only a small minority of successful candidates are found in this way, although databanks have a recognised value for identifying sources which might lead to candidates, and helping to establish the parameters of a search.

Headhunters traditionally have played their cards close to their chests and revealed little about what happens during a search. But, because clients are paying for a service, they have a right to know at any time what is being done for the fee they are paying. This is especially true of the research process, which takes up so many costly man- (or, more usually, woman-) hours.

The client will normally expect the headhunters' research staff to prepare a list of companies in which potential candidates are likely to be found and to establish who is doing the relevant jobs (or has done them previously) in those companies and, as far as possible, how good they are. As soon as the researcher comes up with approximately forty to sixty names seen as strong possibilities – and, in 80 per cent of search firms, the researcher will have already made initial telephone contact – then the consultant can get to work on talking to them and building up a comprehensive and well-informed list of potential candidates, interviewing the most promising and producing a short list of the best.

At which point does the researcher come into the story? At some stage of the client briefing, such as visiting some part of the client company's operations, or only when the assignment comes back to the search firm's office? At which point does the researcher hand the assignment back over to the consultant? When a bare list of names to try has been compiled, or when a list of people already contacted, initially briefed and preliminarily reference-checked has been drawn up?

This question of the role of researchers varies enormously between search firms. For instance, some firms frequently and apparently successfully appoint new consultants out of the ranks of their most able and experienced researchers; whilst others maintain that 'once a researcher, always a researcher' and that research and consultancy skills are totally separate and never the twain shall meet. In some headhunter's offices, research is seen as the backbone of the business, and researchers are deliberately involved in all aspects of the search; in others, they are little more than filing-clerks, and are paid and treated accordingly.

If a client is not sure whether or not the search firm has done a thorough job, he should ask to go through their working papers with them, to make sure they have done a comprehensive and truly wide-ranging search. A client is justified in wanting to know to whom the researches and/or consultants have spoken, to see if all possible avenues have been explored or if the search firm has just run their eyes over their files to see if they can get their short list from their own database. A client should ask the consultant how each name on the short list emerged in the first place: was it from the databank or from fresh research?

INTERVIEWING

Interviewing is a tool frequently used and by almost anyone in many aspects of everyday life, yet it is rarely understood as a scientific and systematic process. In the headhunting context, it begins ideally in the previous part of the headhunting process, at the research stage. Thorough background research on the candidate's suitability for the job is vital to establish the headhunter's credibility in the interview itself. The candidate, who has been approached and invited to interview by the headhunter, is at first in the stronger position within the relationship.

When candidates become convinced of the headhunter's knowledge and appreciation of their skills and achievements, and also become attracted to the significance and possibilities of the opportunity being presented to them, then the imbalance in the relationship disappears. At this key stage, the headhunter takes charge. The client employing the headhunter appreciates that the client can be in a weaker position in relation to the candidate, as the candidate can know more about the client firm at this stage, but a client recruiting via advertising can know only what the candidate chooses to tell. Employing a headhunter enables the client to avoid this weak position from the start.

When does a candidate become a candidate? A working definition could be made at the point when the person who has been approached expresses a committed interest in the offered position, when he agrees to meet the client and when it becomes clear that if offered the job, he will take it.

One problem in this context can emerge in discussions with the client who, despite employing a headhunter actively to search for someone, insists on calling the candidate an 'applicant'. One particular headhunted candidate, on being asked by a tactless and unthinking client why he had applied for the job, replied that he had not, and promptly walked out.

At the beginning of an interview between a potential candidate and a headhunter, the former needs to establish how competent the headhunter as well as the search firm as a whole is.

It can happen, of course, that a candidate will pursue an attractive opportunity whilst disliking and distrusting the headhunter. This can certainly make life difficult for the headhunter in establishing a picture of the personality of the candidate.

It is frequently true that the more senior the executive, the more difficult it can be to build up this picture, especially if he or she has moved jobs comparatively rarely and not recently, and is not used to unfolding details about his or her previous life. It is, of course, unwise to rely upon what people say about themselves in terms of their track record. Especially in the case of executives in the financial services sector, there is often a considerable discrepancy between what a candidate will say he or she has achieved, and the perception of that person's colleagues. Thus, informal referencing is a crucial part of pre-interview homework; and not just talking to people suggested by the candidate. It is not unusual for a good headhunter, in the course of an assignment, to collect nine formal references about one candidate.

Gathering several formal references is particularly important when some are less favourable than others. In one instance, a search for a marketing director churned out a candidate who appeared ideal until one source gave a reference that was totally at odds with the previous three. Tracking down the reason why the fourth reference was so out of character took another nine enquiries before it was revealed that the candidate had embarked on an affair with a secretary which had subsequently thrown his professional behaviour in doubt. The number of references sought is a good guide to the thoroughness and professional standards of a headhunter.

A good headhunter is especially on the lookout for reasons why a candidate left a previous job. Particularly for a financial position the need for unquestioned integrity is paramount: being fired on a morality issue is more significant than being fired on a competency issue in this case. Good headhunters take many references, and take notice of them.

In trying to interest the potential candidate in a position, the headhunter is not always at liberty to reveal the client's name. But trying to sell an anonymous job is hard work, and undesirable for the headhunter, akin to working with an arm tied behind one's back, and clients are encouraged to be open whenever possible. It is clearly unfair to potential candidates to expect them to accept this unequal exchange of information. It can lead to a client losing good candidates, as many of the latter will immediately turn down an opportunity put forward without the client's name. It has happened that when clients have subsequently changed their minds and allowed their names to be revealed – under pressure from the headhunter – candidates who had initially refused to consider a job had expressed real interest when contacted again and provided with fuller details.

Fortunately, most clients in Asia allow their names to be revealed, if not initially then at least by the point when the candidate is interviewed by the headhunter. Some candidates take instant objection to a particular company and do not allow the headhunting process to continue any further once they know these details; grounds for instant rejection range from association with a particular product, such as cigarettes or certain pharmaceuticals tested on animals, a bad name for performance or unethical behaviour, or the fact that the company seeking the executive is on the executive's company's hit list, unknown to the headhunter.

Where are interviews between potential candidates and headhunters held? More often than not, the first meeting will take place in the headhunter's office, which has the advantage of being neutral territory. Subsequently, it may also be seen as the best setting – for the same reason – for at least the first meeting between the client and the candidate. In the case of particularly important senior candidates with very tight schedules, then the headhunter comes to them. Such a candidate could well be a client in the future. Otherwise, an initial discussion, a 'getting-to-know-you' session, could take place without papers in a club or hotel lobby or lounge, but this is more likely to happen later, after details have been worked out.

The procedure at these interviews usually centres around going through the potential candidate's CV, or résumé. The format of CVs most welcome to the headhunter is one where all the dates of job changes are clearly stated. Again, very senior executives can be a problem here: those who have moved rarely, or only internally, may find themselves without a CV at all.

Conscientious and professional headhunters will not take the details with which they are presented on face value, but check their authenticity, even right down to the university degree. The leading headhunters all regard themselves as sticklers for detail in this regard, especially after discoveries of cases of candidates with several CVs, each with different dates and jobs. One candidate in particular claimed to have gained a first-class degree from Harvard. Verifying this revealed that not only had the candidate lied about the degree, but also he had not studied at Harvard at all, moreover his entire career as outlined in his CV was a fabrication. Clients can make a serious and expensive mistake because of this; but this should never happen if headhunters do enough reference checking, and are perceptive during interviews where body language can provide revealing clues.

A conscientious headhunter will not hesitate to drop a potential candidate if they discover inaccuracies and untruths in a CV, even if they are apparently unimportant, because if a person is prepared to lie about such details as the class of their degree, they could well be lying about other aspects of their CV and, more significantly, could continue lying in their new job. Unfortunately, the emergence of firms specialising in helping people prepare impressive CVs may have encouraged the production of less than completely accurate examples.

Headhunters need to be aware of the personal side of the candidate's life, however painful or embarrassing this might be to either or both parties, because this can have an important bearing on the candidate's motives for taking a new job. For example, an increased salary is especially attractive to a candidate paying out large sums in alimony, school fees and/or a large mortgage or bank loan. There is, of course, nothing wrong with moving to a new job for more money, but this should not cloud a candidate's judgement in making a strategic change in the context of his or her career pattern as a whole. A female candidate with young children may be attracted to a company offering flexible working hours and the possibility of working reduced hours during domestic crises.

A candidate without such constraints will have different priorities, and may be attracted to move primarily on the grounds of needing greater – or just different – challenges at work. This kind of motivation can be especially critical in seeking to fill a really demanding and revolutionary new role in a company needing a shake-up. Thus the headhunter is particularly alert to a candidate's attitude to future salary. Candidates especially interested in the possibility of enhanced financial rewards will also want to know about stock options, bonuses and perks such as company cars, education and health provisions, and offers of low-interest loans.

How the headhunter presents candidates to clients has a critical bearing on the outcome of the assignment, especially as there have been many instances of clients immediately wishing to appoint the first candidate they meet, because they like what they see, and often because they are anxious to fill the position quickly. A good headhunter will discuss a range of candidates equally with the client to judge and make a speedy decision.

The headhunter will prime the candidate about the client before they meet, but they expect good and keen candidates to do their own homework on a company through their own sources. However, a professional headhunter should be able to answer questions which the candidate might raise about the client in order for the condidate to be able to judge whether or not this would be a good career move. The headhunter should not only supply published brochures and reports and accounts of the client company for the candidate to take away, to discuss with their partner and friends, but should also describe the client's corporate culture and management style, and real details of exactly where the candidate will sit at work, aspects of their daily routine and, in particular, exactly who he or she will have to report to. This is all vital information for the candidate, and also a way in which candidates can check out both the headhunter's and search firm's competency and the professionalism of their approach.

A serious candidate will be concerned to know exactly what it will be like to work for the client. Defining the appropriate business culture, and how this fits into the candidate's previous experience, is crucial. Companies attach greater or lesser importance to moulding the personalities and behaviour of their employees; those with especially strong business cultures, such as Procter & Gamble, IBM, Unilever and Shell, rarely use headhunters at all. But a comparable problem does occur in headhunting public sector appointments, now increasingly common, which impose constraints unlike those required by private sector business. Recruiting in privatised industries can also throw up complex corporate culture problems.

Sometimes a headhunter will be brought into an organisation with a strong corporate culture which has not recruited outside before, just to check that their people are as good as anyone outside. Headhunters who work on the basis of a fee for work done, rather than on a proportion of the successful candidate's salary, are happy to undertake such work. On the understanding that it is better to go for the devil you know, a client may prefer an internal candidate against one from outside, but knowing that they have been compared within the field of talent available by a headhunter who knows the market well will satisfy clients that they have the best.

In analysing the candidate's attitude to business culture and interpersonal relationships at work, the headhunter needs to gather the opinions of those colleagues that the candidate has worked with. How good was he or she at working with other people, either senior or junior? One particular candidate considered by a leading headhunting firm appeared to be very capable but to have conflicts with fellow colleagues. He had moved at least every three to four years, particularly to overseas or regional jobs and back to their home base, in which he was apparently successful, but there was no obvious explanation for the move in each case. Reference checking revealed that this candidate was weak at sustaining long, productive relationships with fellow executives in one particular situation, and had found his niche as a 'project man'. Although he had not previously defined it as such, the candidate realised that his strength lays in solving immediate corporate problems without tackling the necessary subsequent rebuilding work. The ability to work amicably with others is always an asset, but it is more important in some contexts than others. Professional hatchet-men are more effective if they do not get too close to their fellow executives. A good headhunter will analyse

PART THREE THE EXECUTIVE SEARCH PROCESS

the pattern of a candidate's career and utilise their strengths rather than their weaknesses.

The headhunter, when briefing the client about candidates, needs to know as much about the candidate as possible. One of the most unpleasant parts of a headhunter's work can be having subsequently to drop a candidate whom he had previously encouraged because final reference checking revealed significant flaws.

It is not a headhunter's job to act as God in making a judgement about a candidate. The sole concern should be making a dispassionate match between a candidate and the specification. When a headhunter is working for a client who has never used search before, then the positive aspects of a candidate would be emphasized; but with a sophisticated client, a headhunter might explore a candidate's weaknesses as well as strengths.

This will be summarised in the candidate reports – which should be succinct rather than lengthy – explaining the reasons why each candidate has been put forward. These generally start by analysing and interpreting the candidate's CV. Many headhunters will also be sure to warn the client of any oddities in physical appearance to prevent the client from making a snap false judgement on someone who is exceptionally short, wears luminous green socks, speaks with a strange accent etc.

Once the client has met the candidate, then other methods of evaluation may be employed, including psychometric testing.

THE CLIENT DECIDES

If the executive search firm presents a short list of more than six to eight people, then the headhunter has not done enough sifting to reduce the universe of candidates to a manageable number. Many headhunters think, although the client may not agree, that the ideal search has only one candidate. In practice, clients reasonably want to be assured that the search firm has earned its fee and has really covered the market. Clients are therefore extremely unlikely to be satisfied if they see less than four candidates on the short list. Most clients are not able to develop a good feel for who is available in the market-place unless they see three or four people.

Most clients of search firms are constantly seeking a better solution than the first suggested by the headhunter. If the first candidate presented is very good, then it creates hope that an even better candidate can be found. Although many headhunters enjoy demanding clients, because they stretch their capacity and are enthusiastic about finding a good solution, it has to be realised that 'the better is the enemy of the good'. A client should seek to hire the best person for the job, but if a good candidate is identified early in the search, then the client should be persuaded to move quickly to hire him or her. The disadvantages of not closing in quickly on good candidates are that either they will lose enthusiasm and interest in the new opportunity, or they will be attracted by some other competitive opportunity which may be placed before them. Once the search has started, it is the task of the headhunter to ensure that the client pursues the candidates with vigour. It is by a combination of effort on the part of the headhunter and client that a successful search is concluded. If the headhunter is slow to put forward candidates, or if the client is unavailable and unable or unwilling to make enough time to interview candidates who have been presented, then the search is doomed to failure. The exercise requires speed, energy and enthusiasm on both sides.

A search should normally be concluded in about ninety days. This does not mean to say that the search cannot be done more quickly. Some searches take only two or three weeks, but this is exceptional. Equally, searches have taken very much longer than ninety days, but a client should certainly be disappointed if he or she is not close to a solution after three months.

When a search is very fast, the client may think that it was too easy, and the firm did not deserve its fee. But clients come to a search firm in a similar way that one goes to a lawyer or an accountant. It is not a question of being paid for how long the job takes, but it is being paid for one's knowledge of the industry, and contacts with people within the industry who might be susceptible to a move. Far from being disappointed about the search being done quickly, a client should be very pleased. After all, one of the main reasons for employing a search consultant is to save the client's management time. If the search is done very quickly, the client has used minimum management time, and made maximum saving by going to the headhunter who knows his market well.

The successful candidate who survives all the stages of the headhunting process – including selection by the client – has to meet three broad major criteria. These three criteria have different weights of importance. About 20 per cent is the candidate's level of intellectual ability. This is normally indicated by his or her qualifications, such as having qualified as a chartered accountant – ideally winning a prize or a place – and having a good degree, regardless of the subject of the degree.

Another 20 per cent of the candidate's important attributes are the jobs done which are relevant to the particular client's needs, and this does not simply mean that the candidate was the Sales Director or the Finance Director or the MD. What matters most is what was achieved within those jobs, such as how sales and profits were increased.

But the most important factor in the success of a candidate is the chemistry or 'fit' with the client and the culture of the client company. In comparison with the qualification and achievements, this attribute accounts for 60 per cent of the requirement of the successful candidate. It is also obviously the most difficult and challenging part for the headhunter to fit. This is where a good knowledge of the client and the jigsaw of the corporate culture comes in handy, and where repeat business enables the headhunter to do a better job. A good and ongoing relationship with a headhunter is something that the client should also aim for, for the same reasons.

If the headhunter is recruiting a chief executive for a company which needs a turnaround, then the new chief executive must be tough and prepared to take hard decisions. On the other hand, if the new chief executive is going to be in charge of a group of 'prima donna' types, then he or she should be very sensitive and subtle. If the chief executive is going to be in charge of an international business, then he must be prepared to travel, with a supportive spouse who will be used to frequent absences.

Repeat business is valuable for both the headhunter and the client. If a headhunter is working for an organisation for the first time, then he or she needs to spend quite a lot of time becoming familiar with the culture and meeting as many relevant senior executives as possible. When it comes to doing the second search for the same organisation, then the headhunter can move much more quickly, and with much more confidence, because he or she has already gained experience of the organisation.

In particular it is very helpful where the headhunter has recruited the chairman or chief executive, and is now called upon to recruit the finance director, marketing director or divisional managing director. In this case the headhunter can tell a candidate about the company, and also a great deal, based on direct and recent experience, about the background and style of the chairman and chief executive for whom he or she will be working. The attitudes of chief executives, and often also their family background and domestic circumstances, all have an impact on their behaviour, and the kind of person with whom they would be comfortable. If the chief executives spend weekends with their families in the country, and then come to the city or main business centre and effectively work from 9.00 a.m. Monday morning to 5.00 p.m. on Friday, staying in a city apartment during the week, and not returning home until Friday, they will probably be workaholics, who will expect immediate subordinates to devote Monday to Friday entirely to business.

This is not comfortable for a candidate who attaches greater importance to family needs, but it is a style of working which exists, has to be recognised and is often very effective. Not everybody may approve of it, but a candidate should certainly be willing to fit in with that style, if he or she is going to take a job with an organisation which has a chief executive who believes in it.

Although there are significant advantages to a company in using the same headhunter for all their senior searches, clients often use more than one search firm, in the same way that they use more than one supplier for goods. It has the effect of keeping the search firm on its toes, and may also broaden the scope of candidates who are presented to the client company. It depends on the number of searches which the company commissions during any one year as to whether it makes sense to use one search firm or more than one. It also depends on the level of assignments and the functional areas of specialty.

FOLLOW-UP

The question of repeat business leads directly to the question of the follow-up of successful candidates. Many headhunters follow up the successful candidate – and the client company – at six and twelve months after the new candidate starts work. The six-month follow-up can be a telephone call to both sides, but the twelve-month follow-up should probably be a face-to-face-meeting to review progress. Candidates certainly appreciate an on-going interest by the headhunter and the headhunter can often be helpful both to the client and candidate in letting each other know how they feel about the way things are going. Although many companies have formal assessment and evaluation systems, they often seem to forget to evaluate and assess their most senior colleagues.

The follow-up process can be of benefit to the headhunter, as it often results in further business for the search firm. The candidate who takes the new job, and then never hears from the headhunter again, may well give future assignments on behalf of the new company to other consultants whom he or she believes might be more interested. The candidate who thinks that the headhunter cares is very likely to give the same headhunter more business when it occurs. Even the follow-up meeting itself jogs the candidate's memory as to who helped them get the job, and it therefore inclines candidates towards giving further business to the same headhunter.

It is a good idea for the headhunter to telephone or write to the candidate on the first day he or she joins. First of all, the new candidate does not often receive many telephone calls or letters on the first day, and second, there have been occasions when the candidate arrived at the company only to find that there was no office or desk, or in one case they appeared to have forgotten about him, and the job he had been offered had been given to somebody else.

A follow-up is all about reviewing the success of an assignment. When a headhunter has been called in to find a new chief executive for a business which was ailing or in trouble, he or she is pleased to note the impact the new chief executive can have on a company, and the subsequent transformation of the company from a sick-bed case to a strong and healthy leader in its industry. There is also no reason why, once the appointment of the new chief executive has been made public, the headhunter should not invest money in that company, and share the gain which accrues to all shareholders on the appointment of an effective chief executive. This is the ultimate test of the headhunter's confidence in the candidate recommended.

CHAPTER 13

AN EXECUTIVE SEARCH
CASE STUDY

STAR TV

THE NEW HIRE : Julian Mounter, new president and CEO of Star TV.

THE CLIENT: Richard Li, son of Li Ka-shing and deputy chairman of the Hutch Vision Group.

THE HEADHUNTER: Ranjan Marwah of Executive Access Limited.

Note: Unfortunately, since this case study was researched and written, Julian Mounter has left Star TV. Six months into his job, Australian entrepreneur Rupert Murdoch acquired a majority stake in Star TV from Hutchison, and as a consequence introduced changes in the management team. But we felt that the story itself is still valuable in providing insights into how a high-level search is actually conducted, in narrative form.

151

"I was at a 'jump-up' – a beach party – in Antigua when my mobile telephone rang", recalls Julian Mounter, now the new Chief Executive of Star TV. "People around me were limbo-dancing and playing tin drums. The person on the other end said, 'hello, this is Ranjan Marwah. I'm a headhunter. How would you like to come and work in Hong Kong?'".

THE CANDIDATE

Three months before this phone call, Mounter had completed the major task of turning around a major New Zealand-based broadcasting company, a task which had taken him six years. Born in Cornwall, England, Mounter had spent much of his childhood in Asia, and started his career as a reporter on local newspapers before joining *The Times* of London. "I made it to Fleet Street much sooner than I expected. I was having an exciting, happy life as a journalist. But I kept thinking, what shall I do next?" So he switched to television, first with London Weekend Television, before directing the BBC's flagship programme, *Panorama.*

Mounter made the transition to management with another UK television channel, Westward Television: "I wanted more control over my work, even if it meant going from in front of the camera to behind it." He then moved to Thames Television, and then left mainstream television to become Director of Programme and Production for Thorn-EMI's cable and satellite division. He was then headhunted in 1986 to head-up TV New Zealand. "Becoming a CEO of a large organisation was quite humbling", he feels.

> You're faced every day with very big decisions, and you know you can't always be right. I had to downsize TVNZ in the first two years, and had to lay off thousands of people. If you're at all sensitive it's very stressful, but in any lifeboat situation you have to sacrifice some so that others will survive. But I'm glad to say that we then created new businesses with more jobs than those we cut.

Publicly credited with turning around TVNZ's financial performance, Mounter led TVNZ's expansion into telecoms, pay TV and satellite broadcasting. Now, at the peak of his career, he decided to do something he had always wanted to do: take a year off and go sailing. "Sailing takes you completely out of yourself. You're being thrown around by the waves, you don't sleep but, amazingly, it makes you feel totally refreshed."

Many people wondered what he was doing, including veteran Australian entrepreneur and friend Kerry Packer. When I told him I was leaving TVNZ, Kerry said, 'Where are you going now?'. 'Nowhere', I replied. 'Don't give me that bullshit', said Kerry. 'No, it's true, I'm going sailing.' 'But no one steps off the ladder at the height of his career', Packer insisted. Similarly, New Zealand merchant banker Sir Michael Faye said, 'Mounter's gone troppo'. So when calls from headhunters came, I began to feel more comfortable about having stepped off into the middle of nothing, that I hadn't closed all doors.

A NUMBER OF OPTIONS

"I had received a number of invitations to pursue opportunities since I began my year of sailing. Someone would ring and say, 'are you available?', and I would say, 'it's kind of you to call, but you need someone quickly, so why don't you try someone else?'". But Marwah's approach, three months into his sailing adventure, became something different.

In that first phone call from Hong Kong to Antigua, the search consultant – I hadn't heard of him before – explained that he was working on behalf of a major Asian client in broadcasting. I guessed straight away who it was, but at this stage he wouldn't confirm or deny it. But he led me to believe that I was right, but not specifically so. I remember saying he would have a hard job to get me, especially as I was quite determined to carry on sailing for a year. I went on board a friend's boat the next morning for coffee, and recounted the story of how I'd received this bizarre phone call, and decided, 'why would I want to go to Hong Kong?'

Strangely enough, a week later I received another headhunter's call, this time from a major international search firm who had called me several times before. They told me about a massive job managing 9,000 people, rationalising a company with thirty businesses, based in Australia. I had already been offered a job in the United States, and was later to be offered another, in London. I was concerned that if I kept these jobs up in the air and didn't respond, they may not contact me again in a year's time when I would be seriously looking. So, I responded, indicating that I was busy sailing, and to get me to change my mind they would have to come up with something really exciting.

THE CLIENT

The scene: the 22nd floor of Hutchison House. The hushed corridors adorned with deep-pile carpet and incongruous wood-panelled columns are occasionally disturbed by young executive aides scurrying around carrying papers and files. A small army of messengers and tea ladies follow in their wake. Having created considerable anticipation, Richard Li appears.

The son of leading Hong Kong tycoon Li Ka-shing – well known to be one of the richest men in Asia – Richard Li is deputy chairman of the HutchVision Group, and an executive director of Hutchison Whampoa. Born and brought up in Hong Kong before leaving for California at the age of 13, he was educated at Stanford in engineering and economics, and has also completed advanced management programmes at London Business School and Harvard. A highly international and very sophisticated young businessman, Li enjoys great confidence and support from his father, and is seen in Hong Kong business circles as potentially very much a chip off the old block. Having worked in Canada and in New York as an investment banker, Li returned to Hong Kong three years ago and established Star TV and Media Assets. Chinese, with Canadian citizenship, Li is now aged 26.

"Within the telecom division, we had a pet project started by only six individuals over a weekend", he recalls, explaining the origins of Star TV. "We worked hard on it but we didn't expect too much when we presented it to the Board of Hutchison Whampoa. Now Star TV employs nearly five hundred people at the head office alone, and accesses 45 million viewers – over 11 million households – across Asia."

A FAST-GROWING BUSINESS

Star TV, in only two years, has pioneered regional satellite broadcasting in Asia. By February 1993, its household penetration had risen by 200 per cent over the previous eight months. Star TV is watched in thirty-eight countries, including 4.8 million households in China; 3.3 million in India; 1.9 million in Taiwan; 300,000 in Hong Kong; and nearly 150,000 in the Philippines.

Incorporated in January 1991, Star TV put up its first test signal in April and, by December, had launched five channels: Prime Sports, MTV Asia, BBC World Service TV, the Chinese Channel and Star Plus. By February 1992, 2.2 million households were watching Star TV, three times greater than projected. By July, 3.75 million viewers were tuning in. Meanwhile, individual advertisers have risen from 60 to 300, and events such as Grand Slam Tennis are consistently sold out. When Star TV began broadcasting, there was practically no reception equipment available in its footprint: now, there are over 40,000 cable companies in the region whose primary business is relaying Star TV to customers. Star TV listings appear in 240 newspapers, and its hotel and consumer TV guides published with local partners in nine countries reach 850,000 viewers.

THE OPPORTUNITY

Li has been involved in the management of Star TV since the beginning, but he never wanted to run it on a day-to-day basis. Li has responsibilities as Executive Director of Hutchison Whampoa and as Deputy Chairman of the HutchVision Group.

> I also have a strong urge to participate in Star TV at the headquarters level. But from the start I envisaged that I'd find an MD or CEO, one that I'd be comfortable with, as I would still be ultimately responsible for the P and L of Star.
>
> I had one individual heading Star from Day One, and the position has been vacant since he left. For the last three years, I have been searching for someone to replace him, so that I can lay the burden of management onto someone else, someone I can trust, who feels responsible for and receptive to our viewers.

THE SPECIFICATION

Li originally wanted to find an Asian for an Asian operation. "I considered, he must be an Asian. I thought it would be difficult to find an expatriate whom I'd be satisfied with."

There was a build up to Li's decision to hire the search consultant who was ultimately to come up trumps.

> Broadcasting is a small industry worldwide. I had considered almost everyone I could think of. More than one headhunter presented me with different options. We use a variety of headhunters for different positions. It is a very specific appointment. I always knew instantly if a person would be appropriate or not.
>
> Mr Marwah is a very convincing and effective individual. He knew what I wanted: a strong track record in broadcasting, open-mindedness, the ability to work hard, dedication, trustworthiness, sensitivity to the region, and adaptability. Marwah was the implementor.

THE HEADHUNTER

It's nearly 7.00 pm on a Monday evening, but it could be 10.00 am on a Monday morning. The telephones are still ringing at the offices of Executive Access at the penthouse floor of the Prince's Building. Ranjan Marwah handles those calls important enough to pass his secretary with confidence, charm and humour. He lives on the telephone. "I start making phone calls at around 5.30 am, ringing countries where it's a more civilised time, before it's a more civilised time here. And the same thing happens at night."

Marwah had built up Executive Access from scratch, to a thriving business billing between HK$30 million–$50 million (US$3.8 million–$6.4 million) a year, with a staff of twenty-three (1993 was a record year for him and 1994 has seen a doubling of Executive Access' billings and staff numbers). 1992–3 saw the return of many large American broking houses to Hong Kong, when five leading research heads jumped ship, along with a wide variety of sales directors, economists and others; there were more high-level executive movements than at any time in the previous five years. The most notable move was that of William Phillips, who was then the MD of top-rated securities house Barings, to Salomon Brothers.

Despite the presence in Hong Kong of most of the major international executive search firms, this was Marwah's trophy, bringing with it an estimated prize of HK$3 million for this one search alone. Marwah's competitors are never silent when asked their opinion of him. Those in the large branded international firms feel that he makes up his own rules, and doesn't feel constrained by an established search process which they must follow. They say that his business is based purely on his personality, and cannot develop a lasting brand: he's a one-off. He is seen as charismatic, convincing and effective, but something of a maverick. Many are clearly miffed at losing clients and searches to him, and there's a lot of sour grapes in their reactions.

Marwah's expansive office tells much about his personality. There's the sign on his desk declaring 'Reality is for People Who Lack Imagination'. There are the photos of his wife and seven children. And there's a picture sent by one of his favorite clients and friends – Po Chung, former Chairman of DHL.

MATCHING THE HEADHUNTER TO THE ASSIGNMENT

Marwah knows the media world well. He was a former journalist, in newspapers, TV and financial information services, having previously run AP-Dow Jones and Telerate in Asia. Born in Punjab in Northern India and a graduate of the Indian Military Academy with a liberal arts degree from the University of Delhi, Marwah came to Hong Kong on a ten-day holiday in 1971 and stayed. He rose to become deputy MD of a group of English and Chinese newspapers, and created an ostentatiously successful business in illuminated signs in Hong Kong harbour, known as Media Partners International, later sold to his investor partners to enable him to acquire new businesses in the United Kingdom and Australia.

How did Marwah get into search?

One day I was playing tennis with a CEO friend who was complaining about the trouble he was having with a search firm which was trying to find him a new CFO. So I found him one. He sent me a large cheque. It didn't seem so difficult.

Other major searches credited to Marwah and Executive Access include Gerry Higginson, the CEO of Wharf Properties (including its transport, tunnels and container terminals). Higginson was pulled out of a top government job, the most senior public sector figure to be headhunted to the private sector. In another job for Salomon, Marwah placed Howard Davidson as head of S. E. Asia Corporate Finance. Marwah also headhunted Raj Mitta, the head of the Pepsi-Watson's joint-venture in Hong Kong. His other jobs for Hutchison have included headhunting Nick James as head of Media Assets, and Andrew Partridge as group HR director.

THE MANDATE

"Richard came to me and said, 'I want you to find me the best broadcast executive in the world'," describes Marwah. "He must have an excellent understanding of all forms of the televisual industry. There were important provisos: this person must have true sensitivity to Asia, and he must be a businessman."

Marwah had already worked for Star TV for over a year, and had handled over ten previous assignments for this rapidly-growing broadcasting company. "Star TV is the only regional broadcasting player in Asia, and I've done all their major searches. Hence I understood their style and their needs well." He'd also worked for the parent company.

I knew what Richard wanted to achieve, what sort of person already existed on the ground at Star TV, and what sort of person could fit into this organisation. So I gave him a description of a variety of broadcast professionals around the world, so that together we could sculpt the ideal person.

Despite the great importance and influence of his father, Li Ka-shing, Richard was entirely in charge of the client end of the search. He has a great deal of authority, probably more than any other man of his age – 26 – in Asia. However, having said that, Star TV is only one small piece of the action in the total Li Ka-shing family empire.

THE SEARCH BEGINS

In drawing up the ideal candidate specification, Marwah mentioned a series of actual individuals, discussing their experience and aspirations and knowledge of the Asia region.

> We talked about people running satelite and cable TV companies in Asia and Australasia, and those who had run them in the past but might be now in the United States, Europe or elsewhere. I know Richard had a preference to find an Asian, mainly because of Star TV's footprint.

Marwah explains,

> We did discuss some very fine broadcasting professionals, but none of them had pan-national experience across the region. Richard's requirement was for a well-rounded, experienced, mature broadcaster (Richard used this word 'broadcaster' all through the search) who was familiar with more than just terrestrial television.

Marwah began to narrow his universe of potential candidates.

> After a preliminary look at Australasia, Thailand and Malaysia, I realized that probably my best bets lay in the United Kingdom, the United States and Canada. The talent is more prominent in those countries. But as I combed through these markets, using multicultural sensitivity as a classifier, my universe grew thin. There were not many people with this sort of experience. I talked to several people who came close but upon more detailed reflection/ examination they were more suitable for other positions, possibly within HutchVision, and one day some of these may eventually be hired. But he was still yet to hit the target.

As it happened, Marwah,

> actually knew about Julian before the search began, but I had heard he had taken a year off to go sailing so I had considered him to be unavailable. I know the New Zealand media scene well, partly because my brother is CEO of the advertising agency DMB & B there.

Attracting the Star Candidate

Mounter's decision to become more deeply involved in the Star TV opportunity came with his agreement to meet Richard Li. This initial encounter took place in Toronto, where Li was on a business trip. "At this point, I was, and I was not, interested in the job. But I liked Richard a lot. I felt comfortable with the idea of working with him."

Another important factor was Marwah's persistence.

Ranjan kept ringing me every few weeks. He is not like any other search consultant I've ever come across. Many of them are only interested in making a hire as soon as possible. Very soon – and a long time before I met him personally – Ranjan became a friend. He'd ask me about where I was sailing to, what the sunset was like, and tell me how disgracefully decadent I was. He'd ask about my family. Only at the end would he ask when I was coming to Hong Kong to talk about the opportunity. I must admit that by the time I *did* come to Hong Kong, I was dying to meet Ranjan, and I was not disappointed. I remember our first meeting, over breakfast at the Mandarin. He's immensely charming and charismatic. He's also very straightforward. He's not one of those headhunters who slyly phones up and asks if you know anyone who's interested in such-and-such a job, and then at the end says, 'by the way, this is not something which *you'd* like, is it?'. Ranjan is the human face of executive search, and he's very seductive.

Marwah also showed a flair for imagination and lateral thinking, as well as determination.

During the time he was pursuing me for the job, a number of my friends called me and said, 'I hear you're going to Hong Kong to run Star TV. What a fantastic opportunity!' I have no proof that it was Ranjan who spread this rumour, but it certainly affected my thinking, and created an atmosphere whereby I could imagine myself in the job.

The Role of the Headhunter in the Search

A search firm can play an important middleman role, Mounter considers, because at this high-level, "you can't be seen as too enthusiastically going for a job, and the company wooing you can't be seen as too enthusiastically offering it. But having Ranjan around I could understand exactly where I stood."

Marwah's role, according to Li, was most vital in the early stages of the search.

Marwah put his credibility on the line in attracting candidates at the beginning, because I did not want him to mention Star TV at first. Headhunters can be useful in finding out who's available without mentioning one's name. He could convince individuals to take an interest without disclosing our identity. He found me six to eight possible candidates.

Overall, during the search process, Marwah talked to about forty current and former chief executives and deputy heads of cable, satellite and TV companies in eleven countries. The client interviewed five of them, but saw the paperwork on far more. Only Julian Mounter reached the second interview stage.

The Candidate Plays the Field

Until the final stages, Mounter was also considering the job with the company in the United States.

> This was a large, well established public company with 6,000 people, where I would know more or less what I would be dealing with. I still had a lot to find out about Star TV. In a way, I was taking a bigger risk. Star TV was less of a known quantity to me then.

Mrs Mounter, "Paddy", who had accompanied her husband whilst sailing (with their two young sons, one only five-years-old) had to put up with a lot of uncertainty whilst her husband prevaricated. As Mounter describes,

> one morning I'd wake up and say, 'well, I've definitely decided it's going to be Hong Kong: do you mind?' And a few days later I'd say, 'no, let's go to L. A.', and we'd start thinking about living in America. And then, later on, I'd say, 'maybe we should put up with the rain and cold and go back to London', where we first lived. It's not that I'm indecisive, but each of these options was resolving problems or enhancing their offers. Now, she's very happy being in Hong Kong.

FIRMING UP THE DEAL

Mounter gives Marwah a lot of credit in the task of mediating.

> As I kept working through the different options, apparently unwilling to make up my mind, and even veering strongly towards joining the American company, Ranjan played his ace. 'How would you like to be a consultant for Star TV for the next six months? You could carry on sailing but you could get to know the company'. I don't know if it was Richard's idea or Ranjan's. When I came to Hong Kong in October 1992, this was my role. It was a good experience, and naturally it made me want to do more, and achieve something. It also gave me a story to tell everyone why I was here. Even at this stage, I went to London to consider the job offered to me there, but as my wife and I stood in Piccadilly Circus in the rain and gloom, we decided against it. People in the United Kingdom seem to look to the past, whereas in Asia people look to the future.

What were the issues facing Mounter? What was important to him?

I thought a lot about what had given me satisfaction in my previous jobs. I remembered my first job as a junior reporter, where I worked with a senior reporter in a little newspaper office. He taught me what hard work was, and gave me an eye for details. I remembered working as an investigative journalist for *The Times*, on a story on police corruption, which made me quite well known at an early stage of my career. I remembered a programme we did for Thames TV, looking inside a business, trying to learn why it was failing, and what it would have to do to succeed. I learned a lot, and this was when I first realised the importance of a company having a long-term vision. Most of all, I had enjoyed my last job. It was hell in the first two years, but then it was great, and I achieved the major goals I wanted to achieve. Then I left. It was like a favourite piece of music that you enjoy, and haven't played again and again so much that you get bored with it. I think it was right to finish at the point I did, I wanted my year sailing, but now I wanted a new challenge.

THE CLIENT DECIDES

Why did Li feel that Mounter was especially suitable for the position? "He brings a unique mixture of experience to the job, gained from a career in newspapers, broadcasting, satellite and cable TV. It's a background which will greatly benefit both Star TV and Media Assets in its increasingly exciting future."

Li continues,

Julian worked with me as a consultant for six months, and this was the most important part of the appointment process. When I first met him, I kept an open mind. We wanted to see what it was like working together before taking things further. We needed to have face-to-face contact. It could have been a shorter time, but I was glad to have the luxury of six months to decide. In a very short time, our vision was clear to him. He grasped it very quickly. We want to provide entertainment to the vast number of people in Asia whose disposable income exceeds the quality entertainment services available. The area covered by our footprint is the most exciting and fast-moving in the world. Julian knows what we're doing and what we want to achieve.

Li's initial reaction to Mounter was that his track record was impressive.

I might have preferred an ethnic Asian person if he had the same vision, the same understanding, and if he was the same type of professional as Julian. If all the factors were the same, I would have preferred an Asian. But I immediately had confidence in Julian that although he is not Asian, he would work out. The multicultural aspects of the leadership of Star TV are an advantage, not a disadvantage.

The Role of the Headhunter in Sustaining the Deal

According to Li, Marwah played an important part in tracking down Mounter and keeping him interested.

> Search consultants are not a 'must' but they are useful in certain circumstances. They can carry out an important middleman role. They are good as agents in getting the chemistry right between two parties. In developing a deal, there are certain things a principal can't do on his own. Certain things could be inconvenient or embarrassing. But I will not say unimportant.

Li continues,

> I used to be an investment banker in a leading underwriting firm in Canada, and so I have considerable experience in closing deals. One rule was always clear to me: principals deal with principals. So although the headhunter *did* play a role here it was not, I think, as important a role as in the early stages. But we will continue to use him, as we did in the past, but not necessarily exclusively.

Marwah himself, unsurprisingly, adds to the picture. "The search I conducted for Richard was extremely valuable beyond just tracking down Julian and attracting him to the opportunity", Marwah insists.

> It generated a lot of interest in Star TV, and was a good universe-building exercise for the HutchVision Group. And I would like to dispel a myth about busy people like Richard Li. When it comes to hiring key people, the extremely busy and inaccessible Richard Li became far more available, and we spoke to each other almost daily, including weekends and holidays, about the progress of the assignment. This became more and more frequent as Julian was identified.

This was not the most straightforward of Marwah's assignments, as for much of the deal-making period his target was nowhere to be found, except somewhere on a boat between the windward and the leeward Islands.

Using past contacts in New Zealand who had stayed in touch with Julian whilst he was sailing, we worked a system of relayed telephone calls for a week, before I was able to contact him for the first time, and often subsequently it remained difficult.

Organising for Mounter to meet Richard Li was scarcely easier.

We planned that when Julian arrived on board his boat in Spain, he would go to a British Airways counter to get a ticket to Canada. Richard was extremely busy – as ever – and I had to match his tight schedule flying between North America, Europe and Asia with Julian's sailing plans and the progress of *Pacific Pearl*, Julian's boat. One of my key tasks during this time was to sustain Julian's interest in the opportunity.

THE CANDIDATE DECIDES

"When I returned to Hong Kong the second time", Mounter reflects,

Ranjan ramped up his efforts, and we began to talk about the package. The package isn't necessarily the most important thing, but if it isn't right, this is a strong excuse not to go. It was easier to ask for what I wanted from Richard through Ranjan. There's a danger of loss of face otherwise, on both sides.

Mounter was increasingly captivated by the sheer energy of Hong Kong, and impressed by how far Star TV had come in a short time.

Star TV is in good shape considering it is only two years old, especially when you consider that satellite TV worldwide is not doing so well. I'd not met many Star TV people before, but have come to know many now, and they're very good. Richard and I continued to get on very well. By the time I went to Hong Kong for the second time, we had a contract. But at this level, it's impossible to make up your mind quickly.

Mounter points out that,

Richard Li is an immensely intelligent young man who realised exactly what I was going through at the decision-making stage. It's a very big step. It's only 50 per cent whether you want to do the job or not. The other 50 per cent is whether the job can be done or not. Is the company you're about to go to capable of achieving its goals? Does it have the commitment and the resources? Can it stand up against its competitors? As CEO, it's like buying a company, not just having a job in it. If things don't work out, it's your fault, and this could potentially be damaging to your career.

I also had to think through how this opportunity fitted in with my view of my career. Although in my management style I've always advocated the idea of having long-term goals and working towards these, I haven't really had a long-term career plan. I've had short-term goals and, when I've achieved these (usually more quickly than I expected), I've considered what I should do next. I've been a bit opportunistic, but I've always tried to do things at the leading edge. Going to New Zealand was following the trend of deregulation, and now Asia seems the place to be. Having spent much of my childhood and a considerable amount of time since in Asia, I am aware of the cultural sensitivities of our enormous region and diverse people.

The Role of the Headhunter in the Wrap-Up

"In the final negotiations", Mounter insists,

> Ranjan was there all the time. It didn't seem strange to me to have an intermediary. As a journalist, I'd had an intermediary who'd renegotiated my contract with the BBC or *The Times* every year. I knew the job would be a tough one, so the compensation had to be appropriate.

Keeping in touch with his client, and his candidate, throughout the search process continued to pose challenges for Marwah. In the final wrap-up stage, communication with Li whilst Mounter was in his consultancy position became almost a daily occurence.

> I must have called Richard in eight different countries, including a grillroom in Singapore one lunchtime. He called me at every point, including three times during holidays, when I had to be summoned from my tennis-court by my kids, and climb the 120 steps to my house near Stanley to pick up the phone.

Marwah is coy about saying more about his role in the wrap-up.

> It's all part of the job. It's up to Richard and Julian to go on record about how it happened. The end result is what matters. I have great satisfaction from a successful placement, to say nothing of one-third of his first year's gross compensation.

THE HEADHUNTER'S TARGET

I think Julian is absolutely ideal, in terms of the range of his experience and his regional exposure, and his terrific interpersonal skills. He's the only person who's had tremendous success in more than three areas of the televisual industry in Asia. He is good at mentoring and people development, and has great credibility with advertisers, suppliers, customers – in fact, everyone within and relating to his industry.

Many people ask me about the quality of executives who grab my attention, but I don't have any one ideal. Every search is different. Above all, I look for the person who's the very best at what he does in a given arena. To me, every search, no matter how senior or junior, has to be for a trophy. I have a 2 per cent blow-out rate, and that is 2 per cent too much, as that means two clients who aren't happy. I like to give clients more than they ask for, to exceed their expectations. Understanding the client is more than 50 per cent of the search process.

THE CHALLENGE NOW

The story which began with that telephone call during the beach party in Antigua is only just a beginning. How does Mounter feel, now that he has given up his sailing adventure for a much greater odyssey on dry land?

Mounter considers that,

> In the final decision, when I decided to take up the challenge, my main concerns were: (a) Can Star TV be the biggest and the best at what it does? and (b) Will it be fun and exciting to achieve this? I'm convinced that the answer is 'yes' in both cases.
>
> The attraction of this job lies in the fact that Star TV is broadcasting of the future. My job will be trying to see into that future, to work towards where we'll be in ten to fifteen years from now. I think it's absolutely essential to have goals. One of the most significant characteristics of a successful company is being visionary. At times of uncertainty you must create your own certainty. You must make up your mind where you're going to go, and refuse to be knocked off course. Spending time on proper planning can save you enormous amounts of time in the future. Every decision must fit into the grand plan. You must concentrate on the important, which is not the same as the urgent. I believe that the CEO has to create the environment in which talented people can do well, through goal setting and delegation.

How is the relationship with Li working?

> I see Richard for a meeting about once a week, when I bring him up-to-date on everything. Sometimes we talk about specifics, often we just talk generally. We have a very good relationship. I look after the business, he in effect owns it. I have a lot of autonomy to get on

with the job. He already had a vision, to dominate television broadcasting in Asia. My role is interpreting and implementing this. I don't anticipate a massive shake-up, and will pursue a policy of 'prudent expansion' with the emphasis on quality television which informs and entertains. I need a lot of luck, but I believe that you can create your own luck.

Li does not expect to interfere much in Mounter's task.

If Julian doesn't need any help and produces good results, then I expect we will see each other once a week, no more. When he wants to check on previous experiences of Star, then I'm always available. I think it's important, when a senior person is hired, that one doesn't overide them, unless there is a strong reason to do this. I don't want to breathe down his neck. If Julian is successful, then my intervention will be minimised.

"I have learned important lessons from my father", explains Li deferentially. "One should leave the person doing the job to get on with it. One should give support, but allow him to run with it. I will talk only about crucial financial matters."

What does Mounter enjoy most about the job? "It's creative, demanding and stimulating. It's at the sharp end of my industry. It's the best thing I could possibly be doing right now. It will be tough and will stretch me to the limits, but I'm looking forward to this."

LESSONS FROM THE CASE STUDY
For Candidates

* Approaches can come anywhere, anyhow. You should not be fazed by an approach and think, 'how did they know my name? how did they find me?' This implies you may not be deserving.

* If you're at the top of your career, you can afford to take time off, and you can still get back into the mainstream.

* Search consultants don't necessarily tell you details of the identity of their client in the first contact, but a knowledgeable executive can make an informed guess.

* Don't play around with offers from search consultants. Play it straight. If you mislead them, you may never receive any offers again.

* Don't jump at the very first offer you get. Think about it. Be cautious. Don't give away confidential information over the telephone to a search consultant you have never met. It can make

you appear indiscreet.

✳ Establish from the outset that you can work comfortably with your future boss. If you can't, there is no point pursuing the opportunity.

✳ Establish a good working relationship with the search consultant. This is also essential to the sucessful outcome of the assignment.

✳ Search consultants may have a variety of subtle ways of interesting you in an opportunity. This is an indication of how seriously they are considering you as a candidate.

✳ Use the search consultant to find out about the job, and how much the client wants you. You can ask the headhunter things which you couldn't ask the client directly. Use the headhunter's services as a go-between to avoid loss of face. This is also good advice in the package negotiations.

✳ Keep other options open until you have explored all the possibilities. Don't close doors.

✳ Think about your family and the implications of the move for them. Discuss it with your spouse at every stage.

✳ Negotiate to reach a compromise between yourself and the company. Don't allow yourself to be bulldozed into something you are not sure about.

✳ Think about the company's goals and how it is positioning itself for the future, not just how it is now. Think about how this fits in with your career, long-term.

✳ Understand your role in the company, and especially the part you will play in realising the company's vision for the future.

For Clients

✳ Choose a headhunter with experience of working for you and your company before. A CEO position is too important to take risks with a firm you have not used before. You also need an individual search consultant who knows your sector well, and ideally one who has worked in it.

✳ Be upfront with the search consultant about *why* you are making the hire and what your relationship with the person will be, in the context of the overall mission of the company.

✳ Be clear about specifics, even if this includes nationality. It is a waste of the headhunter's time if he considers people whom you will not contemplate.

❋ Have a clear idea of the ideal skills and qualities you are looking for.

❋ Be candid about the history of the search so far. If you've used other headhunters and looked at other candidates, tell the search consultant. He needs all the background he can get, and needs to know the position from which he's starting.

❋ If you want it to be a confidential search, select a headhunter with credibility and conviction. It is very difficult to interest candidates when they don't know the identity of the company they are being attracted to. As soon as possible, instruct your headhunter to reveal your identity to the more appropriate candidates.

❋ Discuss the headhunter's existing contacts and help him as much as possible with your contacts. Get involved in the search process and make yourself available.

❋ Take time to explain your company's mission to the candidates. How quickly and enthusiastically they grasp this is a good indicator.

❋ Don't be too restricted in your view of who the successful candidate might be and where you can find him. He may not be exactly what you expected.

❋ Use the headhunter to develop the deal. They're the professionals. It could be embarassing or difficult to get too involved in some of the minutae.

❋ Use the findings of the search to add to your knowledge of your business. They could be useful for later searches. They can also tell you a lot about the perception of your company in the market-place, in terms of how potential candidates react when approached. How many of them guess that it is you?

❋ When your successful candidate is appointed, give him space to get on with the job.

P ART FOUR

CAREERS AND
EXECUTIVE SEARCH

CHAPTER 14

HINTS ON HOW TO GET HEADHUNTED

This book is aimed both at users of search and those interested in becoming headhunters' candidates. It also seeks to provide an insight into the workings of top-level recruitment which can help would-be candidates to maximise their potential, and to use the mechanisms of executive search to climb the corporate ladder.

The discussion of the headhunting process and the problems consultants face in pin-pointing candidates, interviewing them and presenting them to clients, gives incidental information on how candidates are identified in the first place and how they are most likely to progress to the short list stage; this chapter will concentrate on the whole question of how ambitious executives can reap the benefits of the more widespread acceptance of headhunting.

This chapter falls into three main parts: first, how a would-be candidate can attract a headhunter's call; second, how to react most effectively to a headhunter's call; and third, how to handle an interview with a search consultant and then with a client. Many of the suggestions offered here are inevitably common sense and not necessarily new but, emanating from consultants and clients, they can be viewed very much as advice straight from the horse's mouth.

ATTRACTING THE HEADHUNTER

The obvious first step to being headhunted is to send in a CV or résumé, but there is always a long shot as leading search firms receive hundreds of 'write-ins' per week. Some firms consign most to the nearest waste-paper bin, but all will retain those that look impressive and interesting. It is vital that this CV is especially tailored for headhunting consumption; this often means a completely different document from that required by an employer or by an academic institution.

A CV will have a greater chance of being retained and stored on a search firm's computer files if it is brief and factual, basically chronological rather than thematic, with the type of information that can be easily entered into a computer and, of course, as up to date as possible. It should be specific about the candidate's principal industry sector, so that this can be keyed in according to standard industry codes. Candidates should investigate which search firms specialise in a certain industry sector, and be sure to target their CVs accordingly. A longer, more detailed CV can always be provided later, and in any case the search consultant will prepare the candidate's CV for presentation to the client.

CVs for search firms should always include salary details and age, as well as any unusual qualifications that might catch a consultant's eye. Although it is always wise to seek advice on the ideal layout of a CV, those that are too polished may give the impression that they have been specially prepared by a professional CV company. Individually written CVs, to a certain extent, is an advantage. And, in this context, each CV should be an original, not a photocopy, and should be accompanied by an individually typed covering letter summarising the key information included in the CV, finishing off with a bold and confident signature.

It is not necessarily a good idea to write to the headhunter telling them that you are actively seeking a new position, but the impression of being open to opportunity should be clearly given, although this is naturally apparent from the sending in of a CV in the first place. It is generally a good idea to send your CV to the search firm's research director, who is usually closely involved in all the searches being undertaken by the particular search firm at any one time, and would know who to forward it to. In any case, research directors receive fewer CVs than consultants, and may well give them more attention. Many headhunting firms include details of their research staff in their brochures.

Although no instant results should be expected, it is a good move to send in CVs to a variety of search firms, both international and local, to obtain a good coverage and maximise chances of being approached, if only as a source. A much more positive step, and one which is more likely to result in contact with a headhunter, is to ask an influential friend, especially an existing user of search, to make a direct recommendation on your behalf. Most headhunters will willingly give time to a would-be candidate who is introduced by a client or a particularly useful source. Again, this is unlikely to lead quickly to an executive position, but it makes a stronger impression on a consultant than a CV alone. Some search firms will give time to 'walk-ins' or hopefuls literally walking in to their offices from the street; but this is not recommended for the most ambitious and high-flying candidates.

Many executives feel that the headhunter should make the first move, and that they should play hard to get. But in this strategy, the potential candidate must become visible and attractive whilst he or she is in secure employment, not when the business climate has changed and they desperately need a new job. John Wareham, author of *Secrets of a Corporate Headhunter*, gives advice on these lines for American executives; the globalisation of business since then has been such as to render his suggestions appropriate for Asian executives too. He suggests ten ways of attracting a headhunter's attention, starting with the need for a degree or an MBA, or both; this is not just for the educational experience, but because without being a graduate, one cannot easily become a member of the business élite.

A university degree is a passport to useful mailing lists in the United States. This is not necessarily the case in Asia, but it is always a good idea to be featured in such lists because they are frequently used by researchers looking into specific industries. By joining relevant trade associations and subscribing to appropriate journals, a potential candidate's name is likely to appear in the initial trawling rather than fishing phase of a search.

Joining a professional or trade association is not necessarily enough; a further plan is to become appointed on its committee. This enables an ambitious executive to become well known among the leading lights of his or her industrial sector, which could well lead to an indirect approach from a headhunter via a source. In addition, it is always a good idea to write articles and contribute short pieces for such publications, which are read by both competitors and search firms. Such work will give an impression of commitment, industriousness and enthusiasm beyond the call of duty, and it is not as difficult as it might sound.

Many prestigious journals and top newspapers are willing to accept freelance material, as long as it is pithy, original, makes a clear point and is no more than 700–800 words. Longer articles are more difficult to place and may wait several months in production. If this sounds daunting, short but effective letters to the press can receive equal attention and are almost as impressive. At least the ambitious executive should be sure that his or her promotions are recorded, and that they are featured within in-house corporate productions (preferably with a photograph), in the company brochure and in the annual report, both frequently used sources for the headhunting researcher.

A final strategy by which to make a headhunter call you, which should not be taken too seriously but may be worth a try, is to return an imaginary call from one, saying that the particular consultant – whose name you failed to catch – asked to set up an interview. This may be dangerous in view of the fact that most headhunters keep detailed records of all their calls, and can immediately summon up such information on their desk-top screens. But it does give you the chance to mention your qualifications and industrial sector. It is perhaps an even better strategy to ask a friend to return an imaginary call to him or her as a source, who can then make enthusiastic recommendations on your behalf.

In the headhunting business, it is not necessarily a disadvantage to belong to a minority. In the United States, by law, minority candidates must receive special attention and some are able to assume senior management positions on these grounds alone and, since it is illegal in the United States to ask a person about their age or background, it is possible to change one's name to give the impression of being in a minority. Such laws are not current in Asia, but many companies see it as a plus to have an international board and one with women directors, for instance. Certainly headhunters discriminate between candidates; clients, after all, use them to find an executive who is ideal for them, and this inevitably involves a preference for people with a certain background, experience, age and sex. On the other hand, a consultant can persuade a client to consider a candidate outside his or her specification because of their strong qualifications for a job. Many successful candidates are not at all what the client first envisaged, especially in terms of age, sex or industry sector background.

Once an executive is clearly visible in his or her industry for their qualifications, achievements and ambitions, and features in common reference sources, as well as having ensured that their CVs are selectively and strategically placed, a call from a search firm is likely although not, of course, certain. The next step is being able to handle that call to maximise the chances of reaching the short list stage, or at least gaining the consultant's respect and interest.

REACTING TO THE HEADHUNTER'S CALL

Writing in *The Sunday Times* in the United Kingdom, Geoffrey Golzen compared being telephoned for the first time by a headhunter as the career equivalent of one's first serious kiss. But this is no time to be carried away, and the would-be candidate should be as businesslike and professional as possible for the minute or so that this will take.

At the outset, it is wise to close the door and make sure that no one else is listening; if in doubt, and if, as in many financial institutions, calls are taped or on a conference line, it is a good idea to suggest a call later or at home. The conversation will necessarily be highly confidential, and it is important for the executive to concentrate on what he or she is being told; after all, this could really be a once-in-a-lifetime opportunity.

It is important to know exactly from which company the consultant or researcher is telephoning, and in this context it is useful to know the names of the leading firms. An executive should ensure that he or she is talking to a trustworthy, bonafide search consultant or researcher. If necessary, the headhunter can be asked to call back to allow time to make checks; if they are listed in this book, or are known to respected contacts, the would-be candidate can proceed with a greater degree of confidence and background information. This can also help a candidate to assess the significance of the opportunity on offer, in view of the fact that certain search firms deal with opportunities at a higher level and in different sectors than others.

Some search firms employ researchers to do the cold-calling only; at others they do all the telephone work. It is crucial to establish then if the call is to a potential candidate for the job, or to a source for further names to contact. Many would-be candidates are convinced that when they are asked if they know anyone suitable for a certain job, the headhunter is obliquely making an approach to them; this is rarely the case, and professional search consultants and researchers would make this clear from the beginning of the call.

Why should a potential candidate help a consultant as a source? Many executives are loath to help in this regard but they may be among the first to hope that someone might recommend them. Even if the job on offer is not attractive, it is always a good idea to recommend a colleague in the same trade who will certainly appreciate the favour and may return it in the future.

Even if your first contact with a headhunter is as a source, it is an opportunity to make a good impression and make sure that you are remembered. Thus the most effective reaction is a crisp, efficient, highly professional telephone manner, which in itself can be very revealing to an experienced consultant. One of the worst – yet very common – mistake that an executive unused to headhunting can make is to ask how the headhunter came across his or her name. Such a question suggests an awe and certainly inexperience of search. It is much better to imply that approaches by search consultants are frequently received and that you are accustomed to such calls. As it is a testimony to your standing in your industry or field, the call should never be queried. If a candidate has been suggested by a specific source, the source's name would only be revealed with their permission.

Even if the search firm is clearly reputable, and the candidate is eager to be as forthcoming as possible, he or she should never give away confidential information. A good executive should show shrewd judgement and an ability to handle confidences. An executive would expect a headhunter to be totally discreet with personal information about themselves, and would also assume that the same rule applies in the relationship between the search firm and their clients.

Other common mistakes made by candidates include trying to play games with the caller, thinking that their value will be enhanced if they appear aloof and hard to get. Many candidates simply do not listen to the nuances and significance of what the consultant is saying, and ask – and answer – in the wrong way by appearing too brash and over-confident.

A call from a headhunter is a time for taking in information; he or she will already know something of the candidate, and wants to explore their initial interest and reaction. Rather than going into great details about achievements and qualifications at this stage, a candidate can offer to send a CV. The candidate should be ready to find out as much as possible about the opportunity by asking relevant and pertinent questions.

The search consultant will not necessarily be able to state the client's name – often the greater the confidentiality, the more senior and important the job – but they will provide information on what the job entails and what qualifications and experience are required; on the level of the job expressed in terms of reporting relationships within the company; on why the appointment is being made and why an external search is being conducted, and on the position of the client company in the market. Is it well-established or a new business, and is it expanding, stabilising or restructuring? What is the company's size, by market capitalisation and number of employees, and what is its current turnover, profit and recent performance? At this stage, it is comparatively rare for a salary to be mentioned, although the headhunter may mention a base figure, indicative that the client has a specific remuneration policy and a maximum figure in mind.

If the search consultant has carried out his or her research properly, some idea of each candidate's salary will have been already ascertained, and that will have been taken into account in seeking to fill the job on offer.

The first telephone call to a potential candidate is the first stage of a sifting process. It should, if successful, lead to shortlisting for the appointment and the next hurdle: an interview, first with the consultant and then, ideally, with the client.

THE FIRST INTERVIEW WITH A HEADHUNTER

Experienced search consultants can quickly appraise a candidate at an interview, but because the executive search industry is growing so quickly, and because a more junior executive may be interviewed by a researcher or junior consultant rather than by an experienced consultant, it is very important to ensure that one is careful to give as good an impression as possible.

From the beginning, the interviewer should be impressed by the appearance of the candidate, who should look the epitome of a rising executive. Too many interviewees wear pinstripes, so it may be a good idea to wear plain, dark colours, to appear generally conservative but with a hint of individuality in a tie or, for women, a tasteful piece of jewellery. Shoes should look clean and smart without outrageous socks or stockings.

Candidates do not help themselves by lying about their salary, especially to experienced consultants who will have a shrewd idea of what they may be earning according to their age and recent responsibility. If a candidate exaggerates his or her salary, the consultant will immediately suspect a lie, or think that the candidate is being overpaid because the employer has not been able to attract others of a higher calibre. The candidate should always be scrupulously frank and honest, yet at the same time emphasize the strong, positive reason for the main changes in their careers. It does not sound impressive to say one left a job because of a personality clash, but if one was dismissed, this should not be concealed; if the headhunter is really interested in the candidate, this will be discovered in any case.

The interview should be taken seriously, but it is not advisable for candidates to try and sell themselves too strongly at this point. After all, you are not applying for a position, but have been approached yourself, and the impression should be given that all is well at work and a new job is not actively being sought unless, of course, you are unemployed, when it should be clear that you have many irons in the fire and that you are not desperate. If this is in any way a selling exercise, it is one by the consultant of the opportunity on offer, not of the candidate to the client.

At this point, the name of the client will generally be revealed – unless the assignment is especially confidential – and more details about the company. If a candidate has very strong reservations about that particular company, such as moral qualms about their products or geographical field of operations, these should be voiced at this stage. At the beginning of the contact between the consultant and the candidate, the latter is in a stronger position, especially until it has been ascertained whether the job is of real interest or not. The best line for a candidate to take at this stage is to be circumspect but not offhand, and to ask many relevant questions.

Yet, oblique reference may be made to one's achievements – beyond the more obvious ones which the consultant will already know about – especially those showing commitment and effort, such as gaining degrees part-time by evening classes. Copies of any articles and corporate material to which one has contributed – as long as it is not confidential – should be brought along. A candidate should appear hard-working, capable, secure, well adjusted and basically happy. The consultant is looking for industry knowledge and experience, but also at the way the personal chemistry between the client and the candidate would work.

Although most of the interview will be concerned with direct work experience, a further sense of commitment can be imparted from one's activities outside the office, especially one's reading: *World Executive's Digest, The Economist, Business Week* and the *Asian Wall Street Journal* give a good impression, as well as famous and important management books, such as by Peter Drucker and other gurus, and autobiographies like *Odyssey*, on John Sculley's move from Pepsi-Cola to Apple Computers. There is also certainly now a very strong accent on personal fitness, and many companies offer work-out facilities for employees. It is also a sign of high level of self-discipline.

At the end of the interview – after about one-and-a-half to two hours – when candidates feel that all their questions have been answered and that they have given the best impression possible, they should then politely break off, explaining that work is pressing, but that the opportunity has been much appreciated. If one is interested in the position, one should say so, but always being aware that there will be many other candidates and this does not mean that a meeting with the client and offer of the job is next on the horizon. It will still be very competitive, and the candidate should be prepared for the possibility of several more meetings before anything definite is resolved. Before an offer is made, certain reference checks will be carried out (and many afterwards) and the veracity of qualifications will be ascertained.

The meeting with the client will be less of a case of giving and receiving of information, because the candidate will have been briefed about the client and vice versa. The format will vary enormously according to the personality of the chief executive or board director entrusted with the task, but if the consultant has done his job properly, both should more or less happily interact together. But it is by no means unusual for a search to come unstuck at the last moment, because the candidate's present firm has made a better offer, or family circumstances have intervened, or the candidate has just decided not to move after all. As Geoffrey Golzen suggests,

> headhunters accept the realities of the market-place but they resent being let down at the last minute for no good reason or without warning; and they like to be told if a candidate has other irons in the fire which can, of course, make that candidate seem even more desirable.

However, if all goes well, it is at this point that the doubtful candidate can begin to appreciate the role of a headhunter, who will be on hand to discuss progress at every stage and may well, in the final stages of a successful assignment, negotiate terms which are an improvement on the original offer. Once a candidate has finally been headhunted – which may occur as the result of the first contact, or the fifth contact, or the tenth contact – he or she will have their own advice for the would-be candidate.

CHAPTER 15

CAREER MOVES THROUGH HEADHUNTING

A Case Study

How can you use executive search networks to create new career opportunities for yourself? According to this case study, once you have made a move through search for the first time, subsequent moves follow. Stephanie Lo has been headhunted three times.

STEPHANIE LO, DIRECTOR OF INSTITUTIONAL BUSINESS, THORN/EMI

Personality

Stephanie Lo is a pragmatic, opportunistic person who constantly seeks out challenges. Nothing is impossible, including being the first woman Hongkong Bank executive to visit Saudi Arabia. Her career reflects her interest in going for the main chance. She is energetic, resourceful, and very determined. She wastes no time in making her presence felt in every country, company and functional area in which she has worked. Her global experience has been a useful backdrop to her work in China, which she sees as of increasing importance. She may be accused of job-hopping but, as she says, "I leave the gold watches to the others." She is open and receptive to networking and new career ideas suggested by others. Her work has been high-profile, and she is known to a number of executive search firms, mostly in Hong Kong but with connections throughout the region.

Educational Qualifications/Professional Training

Lo has an MBA from the Chinese University of Hong Kong, gained from studying part-time. "Maybe a full-time MBA from the United States would have been better, but I did get a lot from this." Lo was originally trained in hotel management and the travel industry, at the University of Hawaii. MBAs are attractive to search firms, who often pick up names from alumni books; being educated overseas is also a major asset.

Career Decisions/Route up Company Ladder

"My first job was not so good. It was a Chinese company, and I realised I didn't like the management style and working within a Chinese business culture." Lo's first significant job was with the Hong Kong Tourist Association, which was a logical progression from her first degree subject. Search consultants look for experience with brand-name businesses and organisations in the early, formative years. A few wrong moves here need not be a major career disaster.

She then made a "both strategic and opportunistic move" by joining advertising agency Ogilvy & Mather, but didn't stay long before going to Citicorp, and was then headhunted for the first time, into Hongkong Bank. These are all good, international brand names which increased her profile significantly. "At Hongkong Bank, I managed several functions: credit card sales for China and Macau; corporate cards; debit cards; and cardholder services, which was the main operation of the Bank's credit card business." She can identify specific achievements here, and the development of specific skills.

When the Bank started an international card business, Lo asked for a transfer to this, and was sent to every location where the Bank had a subsidiary or branch, to assess the feasibility of introducing cards and implementing her recommendations.

> I went to many weird and wonderful places, especially Saudi Arabia. I was told they don't let women in, but I insisted. I was the first female Hongkong Bank executive to go to Saudi Arabia on business. I had to go around escorted by a male employee of the Bank, wearing a long black cloak. It wasn't so difficult: people were glad to see a different face.

This sort of achievement is very high profile and shows determination, drive, and resourcefulness.

Having made her mark during her six years at Hongkong Bank, Lo was headhunted, for the second time, to Rothmans, as General Manager for China. She enjoyed the challenge of selling Western cigarettes into China but when, eight months later, she was headhunted again, for the third time – on this occasion by Thorn/EMI – she took it. Still with her current employer for nearly two years as we go to press, she has regional responsibility for penetrating the institutional market for the rental of electronic equipment and integrated TV systems, mainly to hotels.

Management Expertise

Lo has thus developed management expertise across a variety of functions, including media/public relations, business development, and marketing, in the service sector, financial services, Fast Moving Consumer Goods (FMCG) and consumer electronics, leisure and entertainment. She has always been based in Hong Kong, but has also operated in Europe, the Middle East and Asia Pacific, including Vietnam and China. She sees the common theme of her career as service – in property, advertising, tourism, banking and consumer products – and her principal functional areas as marketing and general management. She knows her skills and strongest assets and has worked consistently at developing these and expanding her range of abilities and experiences.

Management Philosophy

Lo's management philosophy is geared around her need for new challenges, which means she has to discover quickly the most relevant features of a new situation.

> I'm taking on new projects all the time. I try to find out everything about a new job when I start. I'm quite flexible in my management style. So I've been able to work effectively in vastly different industry cultures, such as advertising and banking. If my subordinates are not performing well, I try to quickly find out why. I am not

autocratic, I'm open and easy to get along with. I like to give everyone a chance.

She knows her management style, and she knows the sort of companies where she can operate effectively.

Likes and Dislikes about Career

In her current job, Lo enjoys having regional responsibility and working with institutional clients. She finds the world of electronics and interactive television systems exciting. "TV is more interesting than cigarettes, because TV is a growing industry, whilst smoking is in decline worldwide."

She hasn't found many things which she doesn't like, but in some previous jobs, she felt uncomfortable with the management style. "Chinese managers, and women managers, and a number of conservative bank managers I've come across, can't take my style. I'm always straight to the point. I don't like people with hidden agendas, and I guess they don't like me." Again, Lo is in no doubt about exactly what is right for her, career-wise.

Future Career Plans

Lo is optimistic about developing the opportunities in her role at Thorn/EMI. This role uses her business development and marketing skills, and her regional experience. With the involvement in selling to hotels, there's a link with her first career interest, in hotel management. Her plan is to continue to leverage her accumulated assets, in an environment which fosters more learning and greater opportunities. When recruiters or other companies approach her, she knows the nature of her plans for the future. She knows what might tempt her to consider a change, and what would not.

Advice on Choosing a Career

For the first five to seven years, you shouldn't be ashamed of your job, whatever it is. Use the time to find out what makes you happy, and to help you decide where you want to be. You shouldn't worry too much about your early career moves. If you don't like what you're doing, move on. When you do find a company and activity you like, keep asking for new opportunities and, if they can't provide them, move on.

Lo feels that such an approach is necessary, given that very few companies have graduate training programmes. When they do, there

183

are very few places available. "It's better to get experience first and then try to get into one of these companies, than compete with all the others. My advice is, take charge of yourself, and don't mind change."

EXPERIENCES OF CHINA

Skills Required

With the importance of China to the recruitment scene in Hong Kong, being a target for headhunters means that you almost certainly should have experience of operating in China. Lo considers that patience is most important, together with a willingness to listen.

> You gain confidence and friendship slowly in China. It can't be achieved with one letter and one meeting. And you must listen carefully to innuendoes. The Chinese don't always mean what they say, or say what they mean. But if you have a good relationship with them, they will buy your product or service even if it's more expensive and the deal is not so good. They want to get to know you first. Being a woman is an advantage. There are very few women managers in the China trade.

Language skills are vital. "My parents came from Shanghai, and I learned Mandarin from them as a child. If you don't speak the language, you need two translators, and you don't really know if you're getting the true picture, and it takes twice as long."

Working in China

Lo has never been permanently based in China, and prefers it that way. "There are several things I don't like about working in China. For example, at immigration and customs, they work in strange ways. It's a boring place and there's lots of red tape."

Communicating with the Head Office

Lo advises that,

> portable phones are essential, because once someone is out of the office, they can't be reached, especially when they get stuck in traffic for hours. There aren't enough phones around, only one per floor in some units. It's often difficult to leave messages for people in hotels, because they get lost.

Risks and Rewards of Working in China

Lo recognises the risk of constantly going into new areas of business, and this includes her work in China, "but I have confidence in my own abilities, and it's a matter of finding out my limits." The rewards have been monetary gains and "expanding my know-how. I am not a specialist, but a generalist, as a result of my job changes, and being a good general manager is particularly useful when operating in China."

CHAPTER 16

BECOMING AN EXECUTIVE SEARCH CONSULTANT

WHY BECOME AN EXECUTIVE SEARCH CONSULTANT?

There is no one easy answer to this question. In many cases people have been attracted to the search business through being in contact with a search firm while discussing an assignment they are handling. Perhaps the assignment is not appropriate to them but the managing partner of the search firm may well feel that he or she has potential to be an executive search consultant. However, there are always attendant risks with taking people out of an environment where they have been successful and moving them, mid-career, into a completely different style and sector and trying to make them successful there. Every executive search firm clearly has had their failures. An example of a typical specification for an Executive Search Associate, compiled by a leading international executive search firm is given on the next page.

AN EXECUTIVE SEARCH ASSOCIATE

After initial training, the Executive Search Associate will be expected to undertake entire search assignments with minimal supervision and coaching from the Office Manager and/or Partners. This involves definition of the job specifications with the client; laying out a search strategy with the Research Department, the development of potential candidates through sourcing, interviewing, making a final recommendation to the client; and handling both client and candidate in the delicate final stages of the negotiation to ensure a positive end to the assignment.

Any Associate is recruited with the prospect that he or she will be eligible for partnership after a few years: business development abilities, superior counselling skills in the field and a deep commitment to the firm and its progress are qualities which will rapidly become determinant. Compensation is made of a base salary and a bonus. Base salary is commensurate with the remuneration this person would earn in a top paying industry in view of his or her educational and professional experience. The bonus is discretionary but linked to performance: billings, acquisition of business (new and repeat), and general quality of work.

✳   Age – late 30s to early 40s.

✳   Education – postgraduate degree level from a leading university.

✳   Languages – should be fluent in English, the language of international business. Persons whose mother tongue is English should preferably have another language. An international attitude and frame of mind are important, including an ability to understand, accept and work with other cultures.

✳   Experience – persons who have been in other types of consulting seem to adapt more rapidly to executive search and this is an important source of consultants. On the other hand, consultants from other search firms have very often failed in another firm, but this has not always been the case. Some line experience appears a main criterion. Experience in selling goods is certainly a plus factor.

The candidate's professional career must show a clear progression and unquestionable achievements. Unusual interest, off the beaten track experiences should be of interest.

✳   Good presentation: dress standards of a person working at the highest levels of large corporations.

❋ Above average communication skills: to the point, concise, convincing without being too talkative: a good listener but not passive. Quick to understand the underlying tones and hidden points of a conversation. A good sense of humour is a great plus.

❋ Intelligence and intuition. Empathy and judgement. Good critical mind, but not to the point of cynicism.

❋ Deep-rooted emotional stability. Strong resistance to stress. Resilience. A person who is quickly back on his or her feet after a serious blow.

❋ Self-motivated and a self-starter. Fairly independent and autonomous personality. Achievement-driven. Intellectual honesty. Service-minded and strongly dedicated to solving the client's problem. But not a loner. Capacity to attach to a firm, a team.

❋ His or her ambition should be to become a recognised professional in the field, to handle more and more prestigious assignments rather than to acquire the powers of a line executive.

❋ Entrepreneurial spirit. Good at managing one's own time. A strong interest in people and what makes them tick.

❋ Attentive to quality: high standards for oneself and others. Not willing to compromise with what is merely acceptable.

In the 1970s and 1980s most people who joined executive search firms came from a career in industry. Most were in their 40s to 60s in age and were of an Establishment style and type. In the 1980s and 1990s there are people from a number of different backgrounds, but especially from general consultancy and other executive search firms. Thus, the managing partner of the search firms of the 1980s and 1990s usually has either a recruitment or management consultancy background, rather than just having worked in industry. They are also much younger than the previous generation.

WHAT MAKES A SUCCESSFUL SEARCH CONSULTANT?

Both clients and executive search firms would like to answer this question. The ability to sell is needed, but perhaps more important is the ability to manage client relationships at a very senior level. And skills are needed for particular tasks: for example, interviewing. A headhunter needs to be an excellent listener, receptive, willing and able to see the difference in peoples' backgrounds and how those people might fit into a very different environment. A strong measure of creativity is required, not just an ability to see the obvious.

In addition, a strong administrative capability is desirable in order to be able to manage themselves and the large amount of work, in a quality-conscious and timely fashion. Apart from that, a consultant should have the ability not just to be an egoist but to integrate with a team of people; they should also have the strength of purpose to be able to get results and to keep going through adversity. Another important attribute is the ability to work for long periods almost independently and not feel alienated, but also be able to integrate with the team. One of the interesting aspects of the executive search business is that it has enabled some people, who have not been truly successful at other careers they have undertaken, to be more than successful in executive search. A high-quality academic background, experience in consultancy and line management and qualities such as weight and drive are by no means a total guarantee of success.

APPENDIX

CAREERS IN ASIA

The appendix contains extracts of interviews with search consultants on which careers offer the best prospects for rapid promotion, good remuneration and a high level of demand in Asia.

HONG KONG
Peter Bennett, Peter Bennett & Associates

In-house corporate communications, on a regional basis, is more important for Asian companies, especially the investor relations side. Most companies don't know how to handle financial journalists. A good corporate communications person could get into a line job, and then get more involved in the corporate structure. Secondly, HR used to be dominated by Westerners, because of the insufficient supply of Asian HR specialists, and also because of the perceived value of having a Westerner who can work across the board in Asia. But more Asians are able to do this now. There is less concern with ethnic origins, and more concern with professional capabilities. There is now a greater acceptance of Asians in that role, especially with the backing of senior management. Thirdly, fund managers and specialists in Asian equities are in demand,

190

especially those with a lot of research experience. The emphasis used to be in Japanese and Western markets, but now Asian markets offer good returns. I would expect the pattern to be the same for the rest of the decade, with increasing importance of jobs related to emerging markets, such as Vietnam, Indo-China and Indonesia. Telecommunications and leisure will be major growth industries in Asia.

Banking will continue to decline, because of the oversupply of commercial bankers. In-house IT functions are also being reduced. There was a rush to build up in-house IT in the 1980s, but now it's seen as smarter to use external IT consultants. Generally, the excesses of the 1980s in banking and IT are now being cut back.

People should plan their careers carefully. I always ask people what they will be doing five years from now, and objectively assess their strengths and weaknesses. You should take a macro view of the region, and consider companies where you could make a contribution. Track down prospective employers rather than wait for someone to find you.

Ranjan Marwah, Executive Access Limited

The market is very active right now, and the search business is very profitable. Areas showing the strongest growth are China trade, FMCG, retail and financial services, especially investment banking. A top research person in Hong Kong in investment banking can earn US$500,000. Venture capital companies are also looking for CEO/shareholders to run the businesses in which they are investing. You can make good returns in new start-up companies when you have negotiated a profit-sharing arrangement.

Every executive is responsible for his own career. You must take more interest in your career than your stock portfolio, although many don't. All businesses are moving towards process management, and you must ensure that the process you perform adds value to your company. You must ask yourself, is my full potential being used? Am I still learning and growing? Am I being paid my full market value? Should my employer share his gains with me in a fair fashion? Basically, what is my contribution to the bottom line, and is this contribution being appropriately rewarded? You must persuade your boss to give you an evaluation each year. If your boss doesn't make a practice of this, you should present your own review. If you don't pay attention to these requirements, your career will just stagnate. Otherwise, when difficult days come, you'll be at the top of the list of people to be laid-off. In your career, you can be either going forward or going back. You can't stay still.

Good career areas for the future would include entertainment, leisure, travel and retailing. People now enjoy more leisure activities. Many companies in Hong Kong no longer work on Saturdays.

Anthony Au, Anthony Au & Associates

I feel very cautious about naming the hottest career areas to get into right now. To a certain extent, it doesn't matter what's happening in the market-place. There are jobs which are in and out of fashion, but there are those which last a long time. You should seek a job you like, doing what you're best at. If you're in a job that you don't want to be in, you'll never fulfil your objectives. So your first step should be to take the initiative, go for what you want, and find a champion in the industry you like.

The more promising careers these days are in consumer products and services. This will be a rose garden in the next five years. All countries in Asia are becoming richer and richer, and people want to spend more and more. Over the last two years, Asia has become more and more affluent. Anything to do with leisure and children is likely to make money.

Another good area is training. All companies are short of training inputs, and it is now widely accepted that they need to spend more money on training.

Two regional centres are becoming more and more important: Hong Kong and Singapore. Hong Kong is the focus of North Asia, including People's Republic of China, Taiwan and Korea, whilst Singapore leads the ASEAN countries. Japan is seen as a separate region in its own right. It's impossible to have only one regional centre for Asia.

China is a staged market. The coastal parts are coming up quickly, but the interior of China is for our sons. There is so much potential there, but much of it is long-term.

Unfortunately, some large multinationals are scaling down in Asia, not because they are doing badly here – quite the reverse – but because they are doing badly at home. They are, in effect, giving up the star to feed the dog. They should deploy their resources more intelligently, where there is the biggest market in the years to come. Over here, the ventures are all stars. They may have cash cows at home, but they may be dogs already. If you're in a multinational, make sure it's a star, or you could be retrenched however good you are.

It's hard to say which jobs are in decline in Hong Kong, because it is such a fast-growing economy. A decline in any sector can only be temporary. No one in Hong Kong should feel that they are in a job in decline.

Christine Greybe, Job Access (part of Executive Access Limited)

Marketing and sales are very popular areas to go into, and there is a lot of demand here. Merchandising and trading are also significant, especially in China. We also recruit many people for shipping and manufacturing. The financial area is still good in Hong Kong.

Generally, it is important to be able to converse in Cantonese and Mandarin to be successful in most of the hot career areas in Hong Kong. Expatriate dominance is a thing of the past, but companies will continue to employ them, although they won't be getting the differentiated packages.

The brightest prospects in Hong Kong are in finance, marketing and trading, and in the sophisticated end of the IT market. Telecommunications and satelite TV are continuing to grow, impacting on many other businesses, such as financial services.

To succeed in the Hong Kong job market, you must be able to prove yourself quickly, and make a noticeable difference fast. There's a lot of uncertainty, so you must be adaptable. The market for returning Chinese executives is good. Manufacturing is in decline because of the move to China, so executives specialising in this area must be prepared to move, and will have to be able to speak Mandarin. Mandarin is no longer a preferred option, but is a requirement for the future. Experience of managing Chinese in the People's Republic of China will be very useful. Once you have familiarised yourself with the China trade in an area in demand, it would be possible to reach general manager level in about five years. Those who got into China early are most successful.

You need to keep your eyes open for opportunities in Hong Kong and China. You must keep up with developments in the job market, and build up networks. If you are achievement-oriented and a tough self-starter, you can do well in China.

We believe that Hong Kong is the most active and profitable recruitment market in Asia. Anyone can make a good career for themselves here.

Paul Curley, Q3 Associates

Consumer-oriented positions in the emerging consumer market of the People's Republic of China are seen as increasingly important now. Product marketing skills are in great demand, together with sales and distribution experience, especially if these can be applied to China. The professions still offer good prospects, especially for accountants and medics. There are good long-term opportunities here. Even the actuarial profession is promising, with increased emphasis on developing retirement plans. It's still good advice to go for being a doctor or a lawyer. In manufacturing, you need to be in the parts of the business which add the most value, whether it be making or selling.

Technology has wiped out many administrative and manual information management jobs, and created others. People with a background in robotics are doing well. Those developing bar code readers and other automated consumer systems in leading edge IT have been very successful. The current fashion for ISO 9000 is creating important new opportunities. It could be that this *is* just a fashion, but right now it's a hot thing.

Direct Mail is a growth area, and many people with good experience here are reaping the benefits. Sophisticated financial products and people who can sell them are doing well. Traders and salesmen of derivatives, options and currency swaps are in demand as Asia's nascent financial markets are maturing and developing capacity. This will continue to grow in general, but will be subject to the usual booms and slumps.

Layers of management are disappearing. Everyone has to be making their contribution to the bottom line. You've got to be involved in making or supplying the product or service, or selling it. Just administering is not enough, and middlemen jobs are being phased out. You must be at the coal-face of what you do.

You must associate yourself with where value is added, in manufacturing or selling. You must increase and update your skills regularly. You must adapt to the constant change going on. The specific job skills you have now are unlikely to be the same as those you will need five to ten years down the road. Take a break and assess your career from time to time. Keep abreast of information on pay levels and gain a sense of how you fit into the current and evolving job market. Employment security is now a thing of the past. Too many outside influences are influencing company profitability. Individuals must take control for their own future. However well you perform in your job, some unknown executive in Tokyo or London may just decide they don't want to be in your business anymore.

SINGAPORE
Peter Lye, Hay Management Consultants

The Singapore government and many major companies here are staging a proactive recruitment drive in India for Management Information Systems personnel and engineers to come to Singapore. Unlike many other markets, there is not an oversupply of MIS people, but a shortage. Most of the management positions are occupied by Singaporeans. At entry level, the highest paid jobs here are in IT and engineering. I would expect to see IT continuing to be important in the future. This field is still growing dramatically in Singapore. Engineers are in demand now, but this may slow down.

At senior levels, HR is a good functional area to get into. Of particular industries, pharmaceuticals/healthcare is growing strongly. Singapore is becoming the healthcare centre for Asia. People come from Indonesia and Malaysia and other parts of the region to take advantage of the superb healthcare facilities here. It is growing expedentially, and all jobs in this area will be upgraded.

Jobs in decline include office administration. The days of the office manager are numbered. There is just less of a need for this function now. It can be coupled with finance, with HR, or with other functions. It has become so mechanised, there is not so much to do. All jobs which can be replaced by technology are now in decline. Even accountants, if they are just number-crunchers, will be needed less and less, and will just be checking over the work of the computers rather than doing it all themselves.

My advice on career planning is to say that initially, you shouldn't just go for the money. Go for building up good experience. Try to learn as much as possible in the early part of your career, and don't be too specialised too soon. In Singapore, I'd recommend going into healthcare, financial services, MIS or engineering.

Rodney Wong, Singapore Institute of Management

Engineering is a very good field to get into in Singapore right now. Chemical engineers probably get the highest pay, but mechanical and electrical engineers also do well here.

A general MBA puts you on the fast-track, and offers you greater opportunities. In the next five years, there will be greater and greater demand for managers with international experience, who can look beyond Singapore's frontiers.

Which are the growth areas, and which are declining? Engineering, computer science, architecture are in demand. Administrators and generalists less so. People with non-specific skills start at lower salary levels. Employers pay more to specialists.

Annie Wee, Russell Reynolds Associates

It's hard to say which jobs are good here. In a growing economy like Singapore, many job areas are good and few are in the doldrums. In banking, lots of the multinational banks here are currently not asset-building, so standard corporate commercial banking business is back in the hands of indigenous banks. I would recommend people to seek opportunities in the indigenous banks rather than in the multinationals.

Trading positions in financial services always pay the most here. The returns are visible, so people know what they are worth. If you're a good salesman in securities, you will always make a good living, whatever the state of the market. Corporate finance is still good.

China represents the biggest opportunity currently for Singaporeans. We have a natural advantage. The Hong Kong Chinese may be dominant in the Cantonese-speaking areas, but we are strong in the Mandarin-speaking parts. Singaporeans are going into senior manufacturing and finance jobs in China.

There are good prospects in Singapore in the next few years, for people who are prepared to travel and take charge of a regional opportunity. Of these, there is always a shortage of good marketing people. Meanwhile, the manufacturing base of Singapore is destined to grow more, so manufacturing managers will always be needed. IT companies are still hiring people in Singapore, and there are still jobs to be had in this sector. Healthcare is a good area to go into here. Basically, if you work hard in Singapore, you will succeed.

Li Hsiao Yuan, Strategic Executive Search

The financial services sector and banking have traditionally offered the best remuneration packages in Singapore. This is still the case, but the market is getting smaller. However, the banks are still paying people handsomely here.

The computer industry is still very successful in Singapore, especially compared with the state it's in in the United States and Europe.

One of the hottest jobs here is that of regional, technical marketing directors with multinationals. Regional jobs are certainly the most promising, as Singapore is such a small place, and every ambitious executive here should look beyond Singapore itself. But Singapore is a good place for a regional headquarters, and 90 per cent of the marketing-oriented positions we deal with have a regional flavour. Also, HR as a profession has gained in sophistication over the last five years and is a good area to get into.

Trading is declining in Singapore, and jobs related to this. There was a time when Singapore was a great entrepôt for European and American companies. Typically, they carried out business by appointing an agent, but now the agents are being replaced by principals, mainly because the products involved are getting more and more sophisticated. The trading companies don't have the technical resources to cope, so the manufacturers are setting up their own distribution and marketing systems. You could say that the trading companies have had their day.

Another area gaining importance is business development, especially on behalf of European and American companies looking for opportunities in Asia Pacific. This includes assessing pricing, competitive environments, and mergers and acquisitions possibilities.

Certain other countries are opening up, giving opportunities to

Singaporeans, such as Vietnam and China. Already people are flying in from Singapore on a regular basis. The situation in Vietnam could change very quickly, and this economy could grow fast.

MALAYSIA

Andy Lim, Kassim Chan

Many ambitious executives in Malaysia are seeking career transitions, away from engineering and accounting to more general management roles. They have technical skills already, but they appreciate the need for good general management skills, which will give them the edge. The manufacturing environment in Malaysia is very competitive, and technical skills only are not enough any more. The positions which most need to be filled are a combination of technical and management skills, especially with marketing too.

Some people who qualified as accountants thought they would stay in this profession, but it doesn't work this way anymore. Often, they find they are bored, and unable to participate in decision making, and the trend now is towards getting more general management experience. Many foreign universities are now coming to Malaysia, offering a range of management courses. There aren't enough good teachers in Malaysia to meet the demand for further training, and people are being brought in from outside.

HR is a growing area in Malaysia. The ability to manage people is key, and there's an increasing emphasis on manpower planning, due to the shortages. With the economy growing at eight per cent (first quarter projected GNP growth), the outlook for ambitious executives in Malaysia looks good.

Kian Kok Lim, Hay Management Consultants

The job market in Malaysia is still very good, and companies are looking for people across the board. People have become very flexible here. There are many people doing jobs different from those they are qualified for. I've seen a banker who's moved into a personnel job, and computer scientists going into marketing. Engineers are very much in demand here, in common with other Asian countries which are still manufacturing-based, such as the Philippines. Filipinos are coming here to work in manufacturing.

Technical specialists are still in demand, and accountants. The salary levels of data-processing jobs had fallen but now are coming back. People don't talk about jobs which aren't promising. They're more likely to talk about shortages. One job area which might not be so good is the legal profession, because lawyers are increasingly subject to government scrutiny. Chinese people in Malaysia still find it hard to find jobs which meet their aspirations, and are inclined to leave, despite the shortage.

Employers are concerned about company turnover, although the more blue-chip companies have been able to retain people, more so than the less structured organisations. This is not a volatile job market, but demand is greater than supply, and this does cause some friction. Malaysia has not reached the panic levels of Hong Kong, but turnover is much greater than it used to be. Malaysians must be flexible because of the rapidly changing economy of Malaysia. The job market is tight because there aren't many foreigners here, due to the need for work permits, which aren't easy to get. So we have to rely on our own people, and we don't have many business schools to ensure that management standards are constantly being improved.

C. P. Chua, CAI Consultants

The most popular careers for men here are in engineering, and for women, accounting and administration. Computing is also in great demand, especially systems analysis and servicing, and on the programming side. As the price of computers comes down, computer marketing is becoming more and more popular. Financial services is a bit quiet. Overall, most career options in Malaysia are good, although it's not a good idea to be a lawyer. There's a glut of people taking law, so it's difficult to get a job. I would recommend people to go into engineering. At the moment, there are not enough engineers to make Vision 2020 a reality. I would recommend people in Malaysia to get good qualifications, locally or overseas, to get a better career.

TAIWAN
Chris Traub, Traub Au & Associates

In Taiwan right now, life insurance is a good area to get into. Almost anyone can make a fortune out of this. The market here was closed for forty years, but now many American insurance companies are coming into the market. Services is the place to be, and hi-tech manufacturing at the high end of the market. R&D is good, especially in aerospace, which is now opening up here. Pharmaceuticals is a growth area, and banking, and consumer products. There is a parity between consumer products and financial services. In these businesses, a 38 to 40-year-old in line to become a general manager can make between US$100,000 to US$140,000, with the occasional person making US$200,000. But you can make more than this in insurance, and there are not many Taiwanese who can do it.

MIS areas are still promising, but you must keep up with the latest developments here. This can be quite an exciting place to be. If you have MIS skills and good business sense, you can do well in Taiwan. If you're just interested in number-crunching, forget it. Meanwhile, much manufacturing from Taiwan is moving into China. Low end industrial trading is in decline as the buying offices of big companies are being contracted.

Career advice must be related to the individual. It is hard to give this out in a general way. It depends on a person's training and personality, and the extent to which they have an international background. Now, it's important to think in terms of Greater China, if you're planning to become a general manager. The future of Taiwan is now more and more wrapped up in Greater China.

The most important quality we're looking for is the ability to be intrapreneurial, i.e. people who can be entrepreneurial within companies. They are a very rare breed.

Georgiana Kolenaty, Boyden International

Bankers were most in demand in Taiwan in the mid-1980s, and when the ban on imported consumer goods was lifted in 1989–90, marketing managers were suddenly in great demand, and to a certain extent this is still the case. Merchandising is a good area too. We also do a lot of recruiting of general managers, industrial engineers, and finance personnel. Insurance is very fast-growing at the moment, and people are making a lot of money out of this. Computers is not such a good area now, with many Taiwanese computer manufacturers closing down.

Shortage of good managers generally is a big problem for headhunters in Taiwan. Say, for example, we headhunt a general manager, and then we want to recruit vice-presidents and other people, it's difficult.

Manuel Lopez, Dynatech Associates

The multinationals here are still hiring, but the electronics industry is down a lot. There's a big demand for Taiwanese to go to China, in the middle to senior management level. There's some reluctance to uproot and stay in China permanently, though. Consumer products is a good area to get into, and there's still a strong demand for people for financial services, especially brokerage and investment banking. The chemicals industry is still good here, and pharmaceuticals.

Taiwan is in critical need of competent global managers, who can plan, lead and execute with global vision. The country is growing too quickly for the available people. Taiwan has produced an abundance of technically-trained people, but management talent is thin on the ground. Taiwanese in multinationals are quite mobile, but those working in local companies are very suspicious of headhunters. Overall, mobility is less than in Hong Kong. The Taiwanese family companies are reluctant to hire people from outside their companies.

Vincent Lo, Dr Lo & Associates

There are exciting opportunities in Taiwan in many sectors. Consumer products, banking, and pharmaceuticals are promising. HR skills are in short supply, and so are training skills. The career service sector as a whole is underdeveloped. Our search work is fairly equally divided between HR, marketing, finance, operations managers and general managers, mostly for multinationals. Overall, sales and marketing is the fastest-growing area, together with banking, and these attract the largest salaries. There's an acute shortage of middle- and senior level managers across the board.

PHILIPPINES

Patty Gallardo, John Clements

The sectors which are most active now are consumer products, pharmaceuticals, trading, chemicals, industrial supplies and garments. Semiconductors used to be an important area, but is less so now. There are increasingly more opportunities in marketing and sales, and in HR.

Filipinos are now doing well in software, although they weren't previously seen in this area. There are now some very good systems people in the Philippines, and many Filipinos proficient in IT are active in the United States, Australia, and Indonesia. The Philippines is now losing good IT people in large numbers, especially since mid-1992. Overall, we find that Filipinos are very attracted to working overseas.

Also, new opportunities are coming through due to the interest in Total Quality Management. Many companies are identifying quality managers, and environmental specialists. These openings can help people to break out of specialisms and move into other areas. Present HR and marketing managers can become future general managers.

Glendon Rowell, Boyden International

Marketing in multinationals is the flavour of the month. This is the best job to go for. Many multinationals have a truly international management, and you can be sent anywhere in the world with them.

200

I have exported Filipinos in my work, and would like to export more, as I know they like to travel and do well in other countries.

Jobs in decline in the Philippines include the building industry, where there is no investment, and little interest in the maintenance of buildings.

Orly Zorilla, SGV

We can only really speak for the financial services sector, which is the most important activity for us. We're particularly looking for Chief Financial Officers, Treasurers and Financial Controllers.

Human Resource positions are increasingly in demand, and many women executives are very good at this role. We've been hiring for HR positions here in semiconductors and in the garment business.

There is a great demand for well-qualified people from the Philippines in Indonesia and Thailand, but less so in Malaysia or Hong Kong. At the moment, I'm working on an assignment in Vietnam – a general manager for a supermarket chain – and it could be that we'll send a Filipino there. Most of the middle managers and finance people in Indonesia are Filipinos.

Regional jobs are more and more important now. Managers getting into these positions must think globally, act locally, and strategise regionally. This applies to the top positions in any organization, such as the CEO, the COO, the CFO, and the VPs of marketing, production and human resources. All executives in these positions – or aspiring to reach them – must be able to transact business throughout the region, and move around the region.

GLOSSARY

Common Terms Used in the Executive Search World in Asia

This list includes words in most common parlance in the executive search world, but it must be emphasized that not all firms and consultants use them, and definitions are inevitably subjective and may vary slightly in application and usage between different headhunters. These words do not all appear in this book, but all have been used more or less frequently by headhunters in conversation with the author. This listing is intended as a guide to users of search, candidates and sources. Consultants should, ideally, always define their terms to new contacts who may be unfamiliar with the search process. Some headhunters appear to be trying to blind with science, others cannot see the wood for the trees and simply forget to explain themselves, and many are afraid of insulting the intelligence of those whose support and interest they are anxious to gain. As a result, many people in headhunting may seem to be speaking a foreign language.

Assignment A commission from a client to a headhunter to carry out a search to fill a specific position. The assignment officially begins when the client decides on a particular search firm, and agrees to their initial brief.

Associate A ranking within a search firm, sometimes below consultant and certainly below partner.

Beauty parade Like a shoot-out, but when the individual firms merely display their credentials and argue their case generally, rather than pitching for a specific assignment.

Billings An American term used to denote the fee income, including expenses of search firms and individual consultants.

Blockage A problem faced by a search firm with too many clients within a limited sector, leaving no poaching grounds in which to search for candidates, because too many companies are off-limits or no-touch. This can cause severe limits to growth of volume business for a specialist company and for a specialist headhunter.

Boutique-style A method of approach used by a headhunting firm in terms of clients it hopes to attract and the service it seeks to offer, in the same way that one would go to a boutique for a limited range of quality products of a consistent style as opposed to visiting a supermarket or general store.

Brief, the In contrast with the initial brief, this is a detailed document which acts as a control on the search programme and outlines the expected time-span and the headhunter's fee. It follows the formal commission of the assignment.

Candidate Definitions vary from all persons contacted in a wide trawl to fill an assignment, (sometimes, referred to as 'prospects') to only those who have expressed a real interest in the job and in whom the client is interested. Technically, candidates are just the front-runners, or those who appear on the final short list.

Candidate reports Produced by the search firm for the client, providing background information on each candidate on the short list before the client enters the interview programme/process. They add to the basic CV or résumé, suggesting why the headhunter thinks the candidate is especially suitable, perhaps emphasizing their plus points and minimising their weaknesses, or at least preparing the client for them. Some include photographs; some are accompanied by video-taped interviews, especially for global searches where considerable expense is involved in the candidate meeting the client. Candidate reports are often known as confidential reports.

Client The company, firm or organisation employing the search firm.

Cold-calling When a consultant or – more usually – a researcher has to make an initial call to a candidate or source not contacted before.

The most effective cold-calls follow extensive homework on the person. Often elaborate cover stories are needed to ascertain the name of the person to be cold-called. This is seen as one of the worst chores of headhunting, and is minimised by developing a specialism in a particular sector and, of course, by more experience in executive search generally.

Confidential search   An assignment in which the consultant is not able to reveal the name of their client to candidates until the final stages, making the search process very difficult.   Of course, all assignments are confidential to a greater or lesser degree, and many first cold-calls do not reveal the client's name.

Consultant   A general term loosely applied to all headhunters, as opposed to researchers.   It can technically refer to a senior member of a headhunting firm before he or she becomes a partner.

Contingency-based fees/Contingency work   Where the consultant's payment is dependent on the success of an assignment, rather like the 'no cure, no pay' practice of marine salvage firms in marine insurance.   Contingency work was common in the early days of headhunting, especially in the United States.   It is still carried out in Asia, but most of the well-established, international firms now nearly all work on a retainer basis except for very exceptional circumstances.

CV   Curriculum vitae, known as 'résumé' in the United States; an outline of one's personal details, qualifications, and experience.   CVs prepared for headhunters are not necessarily the same as those favoured by potential employers; search consultants look for very brief outlines in clear chronological order, not thematic appraisals which smack of careers advisors and CV-producing companies. CVs for headhunters should always include salary details.

Executive search   Used in here synonymously with headhunting, but many firms much prefer this more formal and professional label,and never refer to themselves in any other way.

Expenses   Charged by a headhunting firm to the client, counted within revenue but not fee income.   An estimate of the expenses, at least as a percentage of the total bill for an assignment, should be sought by the client commissioning the headhunter. This normally works out at between 15 per cent and 25 per cent of the total cost; but some headhunters have been known almost to double their bills through expenses.

External candidates   Candidates for a position to be filled who are working for an outside company, as opposed to internal candidates.

Fee income   The income a search firm receives from fees charged to the client, excluding expenses.

Follow-up   The period after the successful completion of an assignment, after the candidate starts work, in which a good search consultant will keep in contact with both client and candidate to monitor the progress of both, seen as good for business development, and as a part of the search firm's code of business conduct.

Guarantee Offered by many search firms to clients in the case of an assignment which is not completed in a specific period of time, where none of the shortlisted candidates is acceptable to the client, and if the successful candidate leaves within a period of six months or a year. Such guarantees usually take the form of an offer to continue or reactivate the assignment on an expenses-only basis until a suitable candidate has been found.

Ideal candidate A theoretical person exactly suited to the position to be filled, described in the job specification; drawing up a profile of the ideal candidate is a popular approach to headhunting in the United States.

Headhunting Used here interchangeably with 'executive search', but sometimes 'headhunting' refers to a search where the client already knows exactly who he or she wants to recruit, and merely wants the headhunter to act as a middleman.

In-house recruiting When a client decides not to engage a search firm and tackle its own recruiting problems, either through the old-boy network or by advertising. Not to be confused with internal candidates.

In-house sources The search facilities available within the offices of a search firm, including the internal databank, and as opposed to out-housed sources.

Initial brief A proposal letter from the search firm to the client, outlining their understanding of the assignment, and why the client should choose them; this is followed by either engagement to undertake the assignment or rejection.

Internal candidates Candidates for a position to be filled who are already working within the client company, sometimes in competition with external candidates for the job.

Internal database The in-house sources of a search firm accessible from desk-top terminals on consultants' and researchers' desks.

Job spec./Job specification An outline of the requirements of the ideal candidate including age, experience, qualifications, background and personal qualities. Sometimes also known as job description.

Minimum fee The smallest sum for which a search firm will undertake an assignment. This varies between firms according to the level at which they work, and the search market in which they are operating.

Off-limits/No-touch Companies who are clients of a search firm who may not be seen as poaching grounds in which to search for candidates. Too many clients in a certain sector can produce the problem of blockage, or lack of searching areas.

Placements Successful assignments completed by a search firm, in which a candidate has been placed; many headhunters talk of the number of placements in a certain period as a measure of their amount of business.

Population of a search/Pool of candidates The parameters of the search, the number of people suitable for a position, which can be very large or very small, depending on seniority and specialism.

Reference checks Investigation of a candidate's CV to ensure its accuracy; this term is also used to gain outside references to a candidate's qualities and achievements, from people he or she has worked with in the past.

Referrals When clients will recommend a headhunting firm to another company, and that company subsequently commissions a search firm to undertake an assignment; a form of passive business development closely associated with firms who enjoy a large degree of repeat business. Also used in the context of enquiries to potential candidates in the initial search stages who may not be interested in the job described but are willing to suggest others in that company or among their circle of friends who would be suitable and might be interested, i.e. sources.

Repeat business More assignments and work from existing clients of a search firm, seen as highly sought after since working for an existing client, when the headhunter already understands the business culture, is easier than taking on a completely new client. Many search firms quote their percentage of repeat business. It is also inevitably higher in the older, established search firms than in the newer ones.

Research associate/Research consultant A senior researcher, coordinating other researchers, and perhaps one being groomed to become a consultant.

Researcher A member of the staff of a headhunting firm who undertakes research work as opposed to being a consultant. There are many different types, for example, PA/researcher, research associate, research consultant and research manager.

Research manager A member of staff of a headhunting firm who has responsibility for its combined research resources. The degree of involvement in other aspects of the research process of the research manager varies considerably between firms.

Retainer-based fees Whereby a search firm is paid in stages within the search process, and where the payment of fees is not dependent on the success of the search in finding a suitable candidate, as in the case of contingency work.

Revenue The total income of a search firm, including all expenses on top of fee income.

Screening   The process of sifting through a large number of preliminary candidates in order to arrive at a short list. Some screening may be carried out by cold-calling, or by contacting sources. Otherwise screening may be possible through detailed desk-top research and by obtaining candidates' CVs.

Search budget   The amount of money allocated by a client to the search; an estimate of the total headhunter's bill should be ascertained from the outset. This term may also be used by the search firm itself, knowing that not all expenses are recoverable from the client, and mindful of its profit margins.

Search programme/Plan of action   The entire process of a headhunting assignment, from the initial brief to the follow-up including the interview process and all the research input.

Selection   A method of recruitment whereby a selection firm undertakes the shortlisting of a number of potential candidates through recruitment advertising and interviewing, as an agent of the client company, which then undertakes its own telephoning, referencing and further interviewing. Selection is sometimes offered by marizipan headhunters and those undertaking lower-level search.

Shoot-out   A competitive pitch for an assignment, nearly always at the client's office, between a number of search firms – usually between two to five – whereby the client may judge which they prefer. Not to be confused with a beauty parade.

Short list   The final list of candidates presented by the consultant to the client, all of whom have expressed real interest in the position, and in whom the client is interested. The short list may contain as few as two names or as many as half a dozen or more, but three or four possible contenders is most common.

Source   A person contacted by telephone by a consultant or researcher to suggest a possible candidate for an assignment. This may sometimes be interpreted as a roundabout way of approaching a potential candidate, but the leading firms do not favour this, and make clear when they make contact which of the two they consider they are addressing.

Success rate   The proportion of assignments successfully completed by a search firm. This is compared with those assignments which had to be abandoned, either due to the failure of the search firm to find an acceptable candidate, or an unforeseen change in the job specification, or cancellation of the search by the client. Failed assignments and hence a low success rate are not always the headhunter's fault, but a good consultant will not undertake an assignment without having previously ascertained that it has a fair chance of success.

NAME INDEX

Unless otherwise stated, the names listed in this index are search consultants.

Au, Anthony, 192

Bennett, Peter, 61, 62–3, 65, 66, 67, 190–1
Bhatt, Ami, 55
Boey, Kenneth, 34

Chainarong, 100, 103
Cheah Chew Ping, 84
Choi, Alan, 55, 56, 57
Chow, Ivy, 34
Chown, Alfred, 67, 68
Chua, C.P., 198
Clarke, Bruce, 100
Clements, John, 113
Curley, Paul, 193

Dang Xin Hua, 50
Dollente, Nanette, 105, 108, 111

Faye, Sir Michael, 153
Fifer, Karen, 34, 35, 36, 37, 38

Gallardo, Patty, 108, 109, 200
Ghani, M. Noor, 88, 90
Gielczyk, Philip, 112
Greybe, Christine, 192–3

Hau, Stephen, 55
Ho, Louise, 43
Humes, Alice, 55, 57
Hunt, Bruce, 84

Japp, Ken, 116, 117–8, 119,122, 123, 124

Keith, David, 82
Kian Kok Lim, 197–8
Kolenaty, Georgiana, 199

Lee, Addy, 49
Lee, Henry, 90
Li Hsiao Yuan, 80, 81, 82, 83, 196–7
Li, Lip-Ling, 55
Li, Richard, client in case study on Star TV, 151–68
Lim, Andy, 197
Lim, Robert, 90
Ling, Henry, 82, 83
Lo, Vincent, 71, 73, 74, 75, 200
Lo, Stephanie, headhunted to Rothmans and Thorn/EMI, 180–5
Lopez, Manuel, 71, 75, 200, 299
Lummis, Max, 60, 63, 64
Lye, Peter, 194–5

Marwah, Ranjan, headhunter in case study, 151–68, 191
McAlpine, Kirsty, 49
Mounter, Julian, headhunted for Star TV, 151–68

Ng, Anne, 42
Notowidigdo, Pri, 115,119,120,121–2,125

Ogden, Lynn, 55, 56

Packer, Kerry, Australian entrepreneur, 152
Praptasuganda, 126
Randhawa, Kal, 94
Roberts, Peter F.T., 41, 42, 44, 45, 46
Rousseau, Louisa (Wong), 49
Rowell, Glendon, 109, 200–1

Sathirangkul, Jarunee, 99
Shih, Annie, 42, 43, 44
Stamboel, Kemal A., 118, 119,
  120, 121
Sung, Eddie, 85
Swallow, Simon, 34, 35, 36, 37

Tan Soo Jin, 81, 82, 83
Tan, Peter, 54, 56
Tang, Martin Y., 40, 42, 44, 45–6,
  60, 62, 64-5, 66
Tang, Raymond, 48, 49, 50, 51,
  62, 64, 66
Tee, Roselyn, 89
Traub, Chris,72, 198–9
Tsui, Andrew, 49, 50, 52

Venus, Anne, 88, 89, 90

Vidhayasirinun, Arunee, 97, 100

Wan, Samuel, 32, 34, 36, 37, 38,
  60, 63, 64, 65, 66
Wareham, John, author of *Secrets of
  a Corporate Headhunter,* 173
Waring, David, 49
Wathen, Bernard, 73, 74
Wee, Annie, 81, 82, 83, 195, 196
Wei, Theresa, 49
Wong, Rodney, 195

Young Kuan-Sing, 80, 81, 82, 83

Zorilla, Orly, 109, 111–2, 113, 201
Zulueta, Jesus, 106, 112

SUBJECT INDEX

academic qualifications,
importance of, 38, 46, 52, 57,
73, 81, 90, 99, 110–1, 120
added value of search. *See* search
advertised recruitment/selection
companies. *See* selection
companies
advertising, 134
rates of regional newspapers,
22, 76–7
advice
to aspiring executives, 35, 44–5,
51, 56, 72–3, 81, 89–90, 98,
109–10, 116, 119–20
for expatriates, 120
to sources, 8
after-sales service of headhunters.
See headhunters

BTI (formerly Business Trends)
Malaysia, corporate profile, 93

candidate reports, 146
candidates
achievements of, 147, 178
adapting to change, 194
American and European, 44
appearance of, 177
attracting the star candidate,
158–9
case study of, 166–7
common mistakes made by, 176
compensation package for. *See*
compensation package for
candidates, package
negotiations
experience of, 136, 147
first interview with headhunter,
177–9

initial approach by headhunter,
133, 175
intellectual ability of, 147
interviewing. *See* interviewing
candidates
minority. *See* minority
candidates
motivation of. *See* motivation of
candidate
nationalities of. *See* nationalities
of candidates
personal life of, 144
qualifications. *See* qualifications
of candidates
reacting to the headhunter's
call, 175
reasons for leaving a previous
job, 142
reporting lines of, 131, 136
responsibilities of. *See*
responsibilities of candidates
right responses for, 7
role in the company, 7, 167
specification of. *See*
specification of candidate
career opportunities
best prospects in Asia, 190–201
in executive search, 8
through headhunting, 180
chemistry or 'fit' with client, 148
China
assignments
by Executive Access, 61
by Norman Broadbent, 60
by Russell Reynolds, 60–1
by Spencer Stuart, 60
-based clients, 65
-based positions, growing
demand for recruitment in, 61

China (*continued*)
-based searches, increase in,
59–60
career trends in, 193–4
consumer-oriented positions in,
193
expertise, demand for, 50
hardship allowances for
expatriates, 66
Hong Kong headhunters
recruiting for, 58–9
importance of, 44, 46, 60
job opportunities in, 65, 195
lack of facilities for young
families,. 65
leasing executives. *See* leasing
executives for China
as market for headhunters,
58–68
opportunity for older executives,
65
outstanding consultants in, 59
posting, ideal candidate for, 64
public listing of Chinese
companies on foreign stock
markets, 44
recruiting problems, 66
-related assignments, 30
salaries, 66
searches being Hong Kong
driven, 37
skills required for, 184
success stories, 38
working in, 184, 185
Chinese executives
demand for, 44
desired qualities of, 44
Chinese returnee candidates, 45
choosing a career, advice on, 183
client, 132
brief, 135–9
case study of, 167–8
company's mission, 168
competitors of, 132, 133
corporate culture. *See* corporate
culture of client
defining problems and
objectives of, 24
expectations of, 18
initial meeting with headhunter,
135, 136

rights and responsibilities of, 7
code of conduct for headhunters.
See headhunters
comparing executive search with
other methods of recruitment.
See search
compensation package for
candidates, 135, 136. *See also*
package negotiations
competitive differentiators
of consultants in Philippines,
112–3
of consultants in Singapore, 82
of consultants in Taiwan, 74–5
of specific firms. *See under name
of specific firm*
confidentiality, 131, 168, 176
corporate culture of client, 135,
136, 144
definition. *See* defining business
culture
problems of, 145
understanding the, 17
cost-comparison between searching
regionally and advertising
regionally, 21
costs of search, 20–5. *See also*
search fees
CV. *See* résumé

defining business culture, 145
defining executive search, 11
differentiators. *See* competitive
differentiators
discretion as vital attribute of
search consultant, 134

élitism in top careers, 135
ethnic Chinese candidates, 36
Executive Access
billings, 156
China-related searches, 60
key differentiators of, 61
Marwah's role in building firm
up, 156
research function of, 61
executive search associate, 187–8
compensation for, 187
portfolio of, 187
prospects for, 187

executive search firms. *See* search firms
expatriate population in Thailand. *See* Thailand
expatriate status, allure of, 105
exporting Filipinos, 201. *See also* Filipino managers
exporting of Thai managers. *See* Thailand

Filipino managers, self-exporting of, 105. *See also* exporting Filipinos
final negotiations. *See* package negotiations
financial services
    in Hong Kong, 43
    in Philippines, 201

Greater China
    assignments, 43
    expertise, demand for, 50–1
guarantees by headhunters. *See* headhunters

headhunters
    after-sales service of, 130
    checklist for, 137–8
    code of conduct for, 133
    container versus retainer, 23
    follow-up by, 149–50. *See also* after-sales service of
    guarantees by, 23, 130
    how they get invited to search for a company, 17–8
    reasons to use headhunters, 15–6
    role of, 159–60, 162, 164
    success rate of, 135
    target of, 164–5
headhunting
    in Asia, changing nature of, 18
    how to get headhunted, 171–9
    techniques, 119
Hong Kong
    career trends in, 190–4
    changes in supply and demand in, 34-5, 43–4, 50, 55
    Chinese candidates, preference of employers in Hong Kong for, 45
    Chinese, mobility of, 64

Chinese versus Taiwanese Chinese, 63–4
    importance as regional centre, 5, 38, 46
    job growth areas, 35
    as market for headhunters, 29–57
    outstanding consultants in, 34, 42–3, 49, 54–5,
    popular careers, 192–3
    returnees, success of, 63
    search firms in China, 59
    selection companies in, 47, 57
    succeeding in, 193

Indonesia, 115–26
    academic qualifications, importance of, 120–1
    average salary per assignment, 118–9
    best employers in, 117
    client comments about firms in, 124
    competitive differentiators of firms in, 122–4
    job areas with executive shortage, 126
    as market for headhunters, 115–26
    outstanding consultants in, 117
    proportion of expatriate and local clients, 121
    recruitment/selection firms in, 124–6
    salary levels in, 125
    search firms in, 116
    specialisation of firms by industry, 117–8
    women placements, 121
intermediary. *See* mediating between client and candidate
interviewing candidates, 130, 134, 135, 141–6, 178
intrapreneurship, 199

job specification, 135, 136

Korn/Ferry International, 52–7
    on academic qualifications, importance of, 57
    advice to executives, 56
    client comments about, 53

Korn/Ferry International
(continued)
competitive differentiators of,
53
competitor comments about, 53
consultants' backgrounds and
expertise, 54–5
corporate profile of, 54, 91–2
nationalities of its candidates,
56
proportion of local and
expatriate clients, 91
salary and number of
assignments, 54
specialisation by industry, 54,
88
women placements, 56

leasing executives for China, 67

Malaysia
academic qualifications,
importance of, 90
career trends in, 197–8
client comments about firms in,
92
competitive differentiators of
firms in, 91–2
job areas in demand, 87
job areas with executive
shortage, 94
loyalty of employees in, 89, 90
as market for headhunters,
86–94
outstanding consultants in,
87–8
proportion of expatriate and
local clients, 91
salary levels in, 94
search firms in, 87–92
selection firms in, 93–4
women placements, 91
work permit regulations,
relaxation of, 86
MBAs
advantage of, 99
opportunities in Singapore for,
195
mediating between client and
candidate, 160–1
minority candidates, 174
mobility, 119, 120, 126

of Filipinos, 110
of Malaysians, 94
of Taiwanese, 69, 200
of Thai executives, 98–9
motivation of candidate, 144
multinationals, working for, 200

nationalities of candidates, 36, 45,
51, 56
Norman Broadbent, 31–8
on academic qualifications, 38
client comments about, 31
competitive differentiators of,
32
competitor comments about, 31
consultants' backgrounds and
expertise, 34
consultants and researchers, 33
corporate profile of, 33
domestic/external business of,
32
generalist approach of, 32
international network of, 33–4
proportion of expatriate and
local clients, 37
salary and number of
assignments, 33
specialisation by industry, 33
women placements, 37

outstanding consultants
in China. See China
in Hong Kong. See Hong Kong
in Indonesia. See Indonesia
in Malaysia. See Malaysia
in Singapore. See Singapore
in Taiwan. See Taiwan
overseas Chinese
bringing them back, 62
failure in China of, 63
overseas education, preference for,
90

package negotiations, 134, 163,
164, 167. See also compensation
package for candidates
Philippines, 105–14
academic qualifications,
importance of, 110–1
average salary per assignment,
108–9
best firms to work for, 109

Philippines (*continued*)
  career trends in, 200–1
  client comments of firms in,
    113–4
  competitive differentiators of
    firms in, 112–3
  difficulty of finding top
    executives in, 109
  increasing awareness of search
    in, 105
  as market for headhunters,
    105–14
  opportunities in, 200
  proportion of expatriate and
    local clients, 111
  search firms in, 106–13
  selection firms in, 107–13, 114
  specialisation of firms by
    industry, 107–8
  women placements, 111
poaching, 133
Price Waterhouse
  advertised recruitment business
    of, 126
  corporate profile of, 92
  expansion of, 104
  proportion of expatriate and
    local clients, 91, 121
  search fees, 119, 123–4
  specialisation by industry, 88,
    118

qualifications of candidates, 131,
  136, 198
ranking of search firms. *See* search
  firms
reference checking, 134, 142,
  145–6
regional jobs in most demand, 12
regionalisation of jobs, 111
research, 72, 139–41, 171
  techniques, 130
researchers, role of, 140
responsibilities of candidates, 131,
  136
résumé, 143
  analysing and interpreting, 146
  booklet. *See* Russell Reynolds
  contents and presentation, 172
  who to address to, 172
Russell Reynolds Associates, Inc.,
  47

on academic qualifications, 52
  client comments about, 47
  competitive differentiators of,
    48
  competitor comments about,
    47–8
  consultants' backgrounds and
    expertise, 49–50
  corporate profile of, 48
  proportion of expatriate and
    local clients, 52
  résumé booklet, 51
  salary and number of
    assignments, 49
  specialisation by industry, 48–9
  women placements, 51–2

salaries
  in Asia, 31
  in Bangkok, 97
  in Indonesia, 118
  in Malaysia, 88, 89, 94
  in Philippines for senior staff,
    109
  in Singapore, 80
  in Taiwan, 71–2
salary per assignment, average,
  71–2, 80, 88, 97, 118–9. *See
  also* search fees
search
  added value of, 23, 24
  advantages and disadvantages,
    19
  career opportunities in, 8
  comparison with other methods
    of recruitment, 20–5
  costs of. *See* costs of search
  definition of, 11
  different levels of, 16
  difficulties of, 12
  process, 129–50
  targets, 62
  types of, 6
  users, qualities they look for in
    search firms, 137–8
  users, warnings for, 14
  values of, 6
search consultants
  attributes of successful, 188–9
  reasons to become one, 186

search fees, 67, 72, 80, 92, 102,
105, 108, 116, 136. *See also*
salary per assignment
search firms
in Asia, 5
common features of, 4
in Indonesia, 116–7
in Malaysia, 87-92
in Philippines, 107
ranking of, 14
recruiting for China, 58–9
in Singapore, 79–80
as sources of information about
job markets, 13
in Taiwan, 70
in Thailand, 96
selection companies
in Hong Kong. *See* Hong Kong
in Indonesia. *See* Indonesia
in Malaysia. *See* Malaysia
in Philippines. *See* Philippines
in Singapore. *See* Singapore
in Taiwan. *See* Taiwan
in Thailand. *See* Thailand
senior placements by search
activity, 3–4
Singapore, 78–85
academic qualifications,
importance of, 81
best jobs in, 196
career trends in, 194–7
client comments about
headhunters in, 83
competitive differentiators of
headhunters in, 82–3
employers' preference for hiring
Singaporeans, 82
jobs in demand, 194
opportunities for MBAs.
See MBAs
outstanding consultants in,
79–80
proportion of expatriate and
local clients, 81–2
salaries in, 80–1
search fees in, 80–1
selection firms in, 85
value as a base for multinational
clients, 82
women placements in, 81
specialisation of search firms by
industry

in Indonesia, 117–8
in Malaysia, 88
in Philippines, 107–8
in Singapore, 80
in Taiwan, 71
in Thailand, 96
specification of candidate, 132,
155, 158, 167
Spencer Stuart & Associates (HK)
Ltd., 38
on academic qualifications, 46
client comments about, 38–9
client profile of, 45
competitive differentiators of,
40
competitor comments about, 39
consultants' backgrounds and
expertise, 42–3
corporate profile of, 41
domestic/external business of,
39
generalist approach of, 40
international network of, 41, 42
regional offices in Asia, 40
research, 40
salary and number of
assignments, 42
specialisation by industry, 41–2
women placements, 45
Star TV
advertisers, 154
case study, 151–68
history of, 154
regional viewership, 154

Taiwan
academic qualifications,
importance of, 73
average salary per assignment,
88
career trends in, 198–200
client comments about search
firms in, 75
competitive differentiators of
firms in, 74–5
dominance by local firms, 69
future of, 199
growth areas in, 198
job areas in demand and
shortage in, 200
as market for headhunters,
69–77

Taiwan (*continued*)
outstanding consultants in, 71
proportion of expatriate and
local clients, 73–4
recruitment scene in, 70
salary levels in, 71–2
search firms in, 70
search revenues in, 75
selection firms in, 76–7
specialisation of firms by
industry, 88
women placements in, 74
Taiwanese, immobility of, 64
Thailand
academic qualifications,
importance of, 99
average salary per assignment,
97
client comments about search
firms in, 103
competitive differentiators of
firms in, 102
demand for local staff, 101
demand for Thai speakers, 99
employment opportunities, 98
expatriate population in, 100,
101

exporting of Thai managers,
101–2
ideal candidate for Bangkok, 99
job areas in demand, 96
as a market for headhunters,
95–104
mobility of executives. *See*
mobility
proportion of expatriate and
local clients, 100–3
salaries in, 97
search fees in, 102–3
search and recruitment firms in,
96–103
selection firms in, 103–4
specialisation of firms by
industry, 96–7
trained people, lack of, 104
work permits, difficulty of
getting, 100

women in graduate school
programmes, 99
women placements, 37, 45, 51–2,
56, 74, 81, 91, 111, 121, 201
World Executive's Digest salary
survey, 31